PRAISE FOR *MAN UP*

"The business landscape is always changing and full challenges and risks. In his book *Man Up*, Bedros Keuilian reveals a powerful secret that drives continued growth, profits, and industry leadership. A must-read for all entrepreneurs!"

—Lewis Howes, New York Times bestselling author of The School of Greatness

"Bedros is a master at communicating the leadership skills and mind-set hacks necessary for massive success in both your business and in life. *Man Up* delivers the goods in the most brutally honest way possible!"

—Andy Frisella, CEO of 1st Phorm International and host of The MFCEO Project podcast

"Bedros is an insanely SMART guy. He's a great husband, dedicated dad, and a master at building EMPIRES. It's hard to be masterful at one of those things . . . but he's great at all three! My point is if you want to up level your life and business, you've got to let your brain absorb the things Bedros shares in this book!"

—Shanda Sumpter, founder of HeartCore Business

"From the NFL locker room to the boardroom, effective leadership is the single biggest determining factor for an athlete's or entrepreneur's success or failure. Speaking from personal experience, there's no one more qualified to teach entrepreneurial leadership than Bedros Keuilian."

—Steve Weatherford, Super Bowl Champion with the New York Giants

MAN UP

MAN UP

How to CUT THE BULLSHIT and KICK ASS in Business (and in Life)

BEDROS KEUILIAN

BenBella Books, Inc.
Dallas, TX

BenBella Books, Inc.
10440 N. Central Expressway, Suite 800
Dallas, TX 75231
www.benbellabooks.com
Send feedback to feedback@benbellabooks.com

Printed in the United States of America
10 9 8 7 6 5 4 3 2 1

Library of Congress Cataloging-in-Publication Data
Names: Keuilian, Bedros, author.
Title: Man up : how to cut the bullshit and kick ass in business (and in life) / by Bedros Keuilian.
Description: Dallas, TX : BenBella Books, Inc., [2018] | Includes bibliographical references and index.
Identifiers: LCCN 2018014277 (print) | LCCN 2018021371 (ebook) | ISBN 9781946885562 (electronic) | ISBN 9781946885036 (trade cloth : alk. paper)
Subjects: LCSH: Success in business. | Leadership. | Strategic planning.
Classification: LCC HF5386 (ebook) | LCC HF5386 .K348 2018 (print) | DDC 658.4/09—dc23
LC record available at https://lccn.loc.gov/2018014277

Editing by Ryan Holiday and Jimmy Soni
Copyediting by Eric Wechter
Proofreading by Michael Fedison and Jenny Bridges
Text design by Publishers' Design and Production Services, Inc.
Text composition by PerfecType, Nashville, TN
Cover design by Ty Nowicki
Jacket design by Sarah Avinger
Author photo by Edmyr Barayang
Printed by Lake Book Manufacturing

Distributed to the trade by Two Rivers Distribution, an Ingram brand
www.tworiversdistribution.com

Special discounts for bulk sales (minimum of 25 copies) are available. Please contact Aida Herrera at aida@benbellabooks.com.

Dedicated to my wife, Diana, and our two kiddos, Andrew and Chloe.
Without your support, sacrifice, and patience,
this work would not be possible.

CONTENTS

SECTION THREE: Your Team

PREFACE: YOU HAVE PERMISSION

I GIVE YOU PERMISSION to grab hold of everything you've ever wanted in life.

I give you permission to turn your idea into a business and your business into an empire.

I give you permission to live life on your own terms.

I give you permission to make as much money as you want.

I give you permission to not have to explain yourself to anyone.

I give you permission to be bold and aggressive in pursuit of your dreams.

I give you permission to think and dream bigger than you ever have.

I give you permission to give up mediocrity in every area of your life.

I give you permission to increase your self-worth.

I give you permission to build your self-image.

I give you permission to love yourself.

I give you permission to get what you want in life.

I give you permission to ignore what others say about you.

I give you permission to enjoy incredible experiences with your family.

I give you permission to be a capitalist.

I give you permission to have exceptional health.

I give you permission to cut your deadlines in half.

I give you permission to not just be successful but to build an empire.

I give you permission to man up, take control of the situation, and rise to your potential.

Fair warning: What you're about to read and the lessons in this book might hurt your ego, sting your pride, and even get you to question your work ethic, because they hit so close to home. I'm *not* here to coddle you or to tell you what you want to hear. I *am* going to tell you what you need to hear—to slap the bullshit right out of you and force-feed you the truth that you've been avoiding about becoming the leader that you're meant to be. I'm here to kick-start the life that you were meant to live so that you can reach your fullest potential as an entrepreneur and in every other area of your life. In this book, you're going to discover the six pillars of effective entrepreneurial leadership:

1) Self-discipline
2) Clear and effective communication
3) Decisiveness
4) Emotional resilience
5) Clarity of vision and path
6) High-performance team

Buckle up and get ready for the ride. It's time to Man Up!

INTRODUCTION: BEING A BAD LEADER CAN KILL YOU (LITERALLY)

IT STARTED OFF like any other Monday morning. I got up, showered, had my morning protein shake and a cup of coffee, then prepared to get dressed for the day. But when I went to grab my sneakers, I couldn't find them. I scoured the house and couldn't find them in any of the usual spots—by the front door, in the master bedroom closet, next to the couch. Then I remembered that the day before I had played the drums in our guesthouse.

As a kid, I grew up playing all types of percussion instruments, so when I got some money together I bought myself a used drum set and put it in the guesthouse, far enough away from my family that I could make as much noise as I wanted. From time to time I'd head up there and rock out. I prefer to play the drums barefoot, so Sunday I'd taken my sneakers off and went at it. When I was done, I left them behind and walked down the stairs, across the pool deck, and to the main house barefoot, like I sometimes do.

I retraced my steps—across the pool deck, up the stairs, into the guesthouse—and there they were, right where I had left them. As I bent down to put my sneakers on, I felt my chest tighten and convulse. My chest felt so constricted that I thought an angry silverback gorilla was giving me a bear hug. My arms went numb and started to tingle, my throat began to close, and it got increasingly difficult to catch my next breath.

As hard as I tried, I could barely stand. The whole world was in tunnel vision and the only thing I could hear was the sloshing beat of my racing heart as the blood was unsuccessfully attempting to pump through my body. I staggered, my hearing got muffled, and my chest got even tighter.

My first thought was what anyone's first thought would have been: *Holy shit, I'm having a heart attack!* I was convinced I was going to die. I remember feeling so sorry for my wife and my seven-year-old son and my five-year-old daughter. I felt heartbroken for them. I thought, *Will my kids grow up thinking that working too hard killed their dad?* They were going to be left alone and all for what? Dad's ambitions? Dad's workaholism?

What I was afraid of most was this sense of my kids losing their father and the trauma and life imbalance they would have as a result. I wondered about what man would replace me as a husband and father. What lessons would he teach my kids? Would he walk my daughter down the aisle at her wedding? It all happened in a flash, but those memories remain vivid to me even to this day.

Then I thought: *If I die here, no one is going to find my body for days.* I needed to get downstairs and back into the main house or at least the pool deck. There was a chance that my wife would see my dying body from any one of our massive windows or French doors that are facing the pool deck and call for help.

I stumbled my way down the staircase and to my surprise my breathing eased up a bit. I was able to catch a decent gulp of air. My tunnel vision went away. Then my hearing went back to normal. After that my heart stopped racing and slowly regained a normal rhythm. By the time I reached the bottom of the guesthouse staircase, my "heart attack" had mysteriously disappeared. I found myself in a sweaty mess, shaken up, and wondering, *What the fuck just happened to me?*

Now I know what you're thinking: This is the point in the story when I immediately go to my doctor, he tells me what happened, and

I clean up my life. Right? Wrong. Instead I thought *I just cheated death, and I still have a ton of work to do today and I need to get going.* Monday morning heart attack? Just a little hiccup. Better get back to it now that things were back to normal.

So I went to work like nothing happened. When I returned home that night, I told my wife, Diana, about my brush with death in the guesthouse earlier that morning. Di suggested, wisely and firmly, that I go see the doctor the next morning. After a gamut of tests, the doctor reported that my heart was fine and, in fact, I had not had a heart attack at all. It was instead a massive and severe anxiety attack—the first of many to come.

It didn't come as too much of a shock. I'd been surfing on a wave of worry and stress for a long time. I was a bad sleeper because I always had so much business stuff on my mind, and I remedied that with a nightly dose of NyQuil and leftover Vicodin from a knee surgery I had a few years earlier. The NyQuil and Vicodin combo led to my waking up foggy headed, remembering my reality, and then reluctantly pulling myself out of bed. To remedy the fogginess and regain my energy, I'd drink a ton of coffee in the morning and then maintain a constant drip of pre-workout energy drinks all day. I told the doctor all of that and he was blunt: "Bedros, you've got to do something about your stress, or you may very well end up back here with a real heart attack—one you'll be lucky to survive." I was thirty-eight years old and flirting with medical problems that affect people decades older than me.

This was doubly embarrassing because, to look at me, I appeared to be the last person on earth who would have a heart attack at the age of thirty-eight. I worked out religiously; I went on long, strenuous hikes; I took on challenges in which I trained for a discipline and then competed in that sport at the end of the training cycle. Having never been a fan of running, I once trained for only six weeks and then ran the San Diego Marathon—26.2 miles. Two weeks later, I started a new six-week challenge.

I didn't stumble upon these physical challenges by accident or whimsy: I worked hard to make sure my body *was* hard. These weren't just personal pursuits or vanity exercises. Seventeen years earlier, I got certified as a personal trainer. I was in the business of getting people in the best shape of their lives. I'd changed literally thousands of physiques, taking many people from the worst shape of their lives to peak performance. Fitness and health was my life. If I wasn't training clients, I was working out. I believed I was the poster boy for health and fitness—and I was, but only on the surface. I was physically healthy, but emotionally I was a wreck, and my doctor let me know how related these two things are.

The cause of my stress and emotional turmoil was my business, which was bleeding money, out of control, and sinking faster than the *Titanic*. Years after becoming a personal trainer, my small business grew into a big business. First I started coaching and consulting personal trainers and gym owners who wanted to grow their businesses and become more successful. Then in 2010, I came up with the idea of starting an international fitness franchise, now known as Fit Body Boot Camp (FBBC). It's a group-based personal training program that makes working out with a personal trainer affordable and convenient. FBBC is known for its thirty-minute "Afterburn" workouts—High-Intensity Interval Training (HIIT) exercises that deliver fat loss results, tone your entire body, and are perfect for all fitness levels.

The idea was great, but the business wasn't on steady ground at the time. I had a business partner who was driving me crazy and causing problems for our clients and employees. I had employees who I suspected were actively trying to undermine my business, destroy our brand, and permanently ruin my reputation in my industry. And every day there were more and more competitors trying to chip away at our potential market share. By late 2012, all of that had left me with enough stress to cause an anxiety attack so serious that I thought I had suffered a massive heart attack with my life flashing before my eyes.

But this was hardly visible to anyone else. From the outside, I looked like I was in control and that my consulting and franchise business was thriving. But on the inside, I felt like an imposter. I was bracing for the inevitable crash. I had lost all control of my business. During a good month, my business would make some profit, but most months my business was a speeding train that was quickly running out of tracks. And worse, it felt as though there was nothing I could do about it. Clients and customers started abandoning the business so quickly that I had to empty my personal savings account just to keep up with payroll. When we still didn't have enough money to pay our taxes and run the payroll for our employees, I sold my beloved Nissan GTR just to get some quick cash to make ends meet.

Nissan designed the GTR to be the Lamborghini killer. It was a beast of a car. It was an "affordable supercar." I thought I could afford it, because I thought my income was on the upswing. Not only that: I'd spent more than $20,000 to upgrade the car's performance by adding every feature you could to increase boost, torque, horsepower, and top-end speed. I couldn't afford to pay for it in full so I took a shortcut, put a down payment on it, and financed the rest. So it wasn't a big surprise that when our financial troubles started I had to get rid of it.

I still miss that damn car. My son, Andrew, cried the day I sold it because he loved the times we spent together in it. We'd hop into the GTR and zip up and down the highway at high speeds, winning races against tricked-out supercars and motorcycles. His favorite part of the whole thing was when I'd say, "Okay, buddy, why don't you put the car into race mode, and let's see what she can really do." Andrew would lean forward from his seat and flick all three switches—traction control, suspension, and gear box—into "race mode," turning an already fast race car into Godzilla, which the GTR was nicknamed by the engineer who created it. Zero to 60 mph in under three seconds! "Gun it, Daddy," Andrew would say before I'd launch the car down the road, hitting triple-digit speeds.

The night before we sold the car to a collector from San Francisco, Andrew and I took it on the highway for one last ride. During the drive back home, I looked over at him, and he had tears coming down his cheeks. One of the worst memories of my life was trying to explain to my seven-year-old why Daddy had to sell our GTR so that he could make his quarterly taxes and payroll that month. Kids shouldn't have to be concerned about things like quarterly taxes and payroll.

I felt hopeless and worthless. Looking back at that time in my life, I was in a dark place. I was probably depressed. I did all I could xviii / Introduction: Being a Bad Leader Can Kill You (Literally)

to avoid work. I slept in every morning, not wanting to face my business troubles. When the alarm went off, I'd hit snooze a minimum
of three times. All I wanted to do was avoid my clients and customers who complained about one thing after another. I found excuses
to not be around my business partner because I harbored so much
resentment toward him. Avoidance isn't a strategy—but I was trying
to turn it into one.

As anyone who has been in business knows, what happens at
the office doesn't stay at the office. I avoided talking to my wife
about our business because I dreaded telling her that I didn't know
where the next sale or income opportunity would come from. Few
things make you feel like more of a loser of a man than admitting
to your wife that you're unable to make payroll, quarterly taxes, or
the mortgage. Every month I had to choose which bill I wanted to
pay and then figure out how to deal with the rest of the money that
I owed. I seriously considered selling a kidney.

Everything above led me to that Monday morning in 2012, to the
heart-attack-that-never-was, and to the doctor's office, where a guy
in a lab coat told me, essentially, that avoiding all my problems and
failing to take leadership would put me in an early grave. It was an
alarm I couldn't snooze out of.

▶ ▶ ◀ ◀

Here's what I knew: My business might have been falling apart, but
it was built on a solid idea. I knew it had amazing potential, yet I just
couldn't figure out how to make the leap. Hell, even a small hop in
the right direction would have been nice. But I kept telling myself
it wasn't my fault. I had a bad partner, lazy employees, and needy
clients—at least that's what I had convinced myself of.

When you're sitting on the doctor's examining table with wires
hanging off you, being tested for signs of a heart attack, none of
that matters. Bad partners, lazy employees, and needy clients didn't
land me in front of a doctor—I did. It was *my* fault. I had made
myself a victim by placing my problems at everyone else's feet,
instead of where they belonged: mine. Leaving the doctor's office,

I was grateful—grateful that I didn't have a heart attack and even more grateful that I finally knew *I* was the source of my problems. By accepting that, I had finally gained a sense of control for the first time in my entrepreneurial career—and with control comes clarity.

After that day, I made the commitment to man up as a leader and an entrepreneur. I decided then that "manning up" meant getting disciplined about my physical *and* mental health, leading effectively, setting a clear vision for my organization, communicating clearly and with honesty, and building a high-performance team around me to make that vision a reality. This decision led to a transformative personal journey, and it's why you're holding this book in your hands right now.

It's also what led me to business success. Although I couldn't have known it at the time, the process that started with the anxiety attack led me to improve myself, which catapulted my business. FBBC has since been twice listed on the Inc. 5000 list of the fastest growing businesses in the world, named as one of the top fifteen franchises in the industry, and is listed on *Entrepreneur* magazine's 500 fastest growing franchises. None of this was a coincidence. By making the decision to man up, I went from owning a business that was hemorrhaging money and quickly failing to one that is now a recognized fitness brand and generates tens of millions of dollars per year. I went from owning a business that delivered crap for service and was sure to go under to one that's *changing* the fitness industry and positively impacting tens of millions of people every single day. I can't be prouder of how much I've improved myself and my business, helping others in turn—and now I want to help you accomplish *your* dreams. I'm going to teach you how to man up, too.

MANNING UP

We've all heard the phrase "man up."

*Dude, **man up** and go after the girl of your dreams.*
*Hey, **man up** and go talk to your boss about that raise.*
***Man up** and do the right thing!*

I want to make a few things clear:

1) Manning up isn't something you do in an instant. Yeah, you can summon some temporary courage and take action, but it'll last only a moment and then you'll be back to your old self. Manning up is about building the belief systems, habits, practices, expectations, and disciplines that allow you to become the best version of yourself—to reach your fullest potential in every category of your life.

2) Women can man up, too. Make no mistake, manning up is not gender specific. Most people fail to realize that humans are at the top of the food chain. We have a greater purpose on this planet. In fact, we have a responsibility to this planet, to the people on it, to our families, and to ourselves. Nearly all of us are capable of earning more, doing more, and giving more to the charities and causes that we believe in.

I'm often shocked when I see people living subpar lives: in debt, depressed, in poor health, overweight, in broken relationships, in failing businesses that have such great potential. Why? In many cases, it's because they've chosen to accept mediocrity and prefer to blame others and make excuses.

I'm sure you'd agree that most of us rarely reach our fullest potential in business, health, mind-set, or our relationships, right? What if we actually did the work to become the best versions of ourselves? That to me is what "man up" is all about—HUMANing up. It is a state of mind. It's a way of thinking, operating, living, and being. It's a constant pursuit of our best selves—to reach our highest capacity and become the people that we were meant to be. So stop making excuses, take control of your situation, and rise to your potential.

3) Manning up isn't just about work. Manning up is about owning *every* part of your life. Every single thing in our daily life affects everything else. If you have an argument with your significant other in the morning, it'll still be there lingering in your head in the afternoon. If you get crappy sleep, your day is shot. In the same way, manning up isn't just about killing it from 9 to 5; it's about

bringing that same intensity, energy, instinct, and enthusiasm to your 5 to 9, too.

For me, the process of manning up began after my anxiety attack in the guesthouse. To the casual observer it may look simple: I took a good hard look at the different parts of my life and started working on them. But underneath, it was a profound journey of discovery and self-examination. I read hundreds of books on self-development and improvement. I worked on building my self-esteem: how I felt about myself as well as my self-image; how I saw myself and how I thought others viewed me. I talked to dozens of coaches, mentors, and friends asking for their brutal feedback. I went to therapy and took a deep dive into my emotional state. I got into masterminds coaching programs—groups of like-minded entrepreneurs who want to improve and grow in areas of marketing, sales, profits, productivity, time management, and impact. I kept journals and studied my behavior, thought patterns, feelings, emotions, and actions. I went down some successful paths in my quest and some blind alleys. I tried experiment after experiment. And all of that—what worked and what didn't, what helped and what hurt—is in this book.

Why "man up"? As I left the doctor's office after that massive anxiety attack, I kept repeating it to myself over and over, thinking: *It's time to man up. I am done making excuses. I am done giving control to others and looking at myself as the victim. I know I can do better with my business, my leadership, and my health, and I am determined to rise to my potential. It's time to man up.*

"Man up" was something I used a long time ago to motivate myself to action during workouts. Sometimes, in the middle of a grueling workout set, I'd just say to myself, "It's time to man up, dude!" And then I'd get under the bar and squat, press, or pull my heaviest weight, setting a PR (personal record). That might seem like a small thing—except that, for me, "It's time to man up" became a code, a reminder that I was going to make my best effort to fix what was wrong with myself and my business. It was a reminder that I had to stop making excuses and take control.

Mantras can get a bad rap. People often think that just because something is quick, it's ineffective. Quite the opposite: Sometimes the best tool for the job is the one that you can use quickly and easily without having too much time to overthink it or get lost in procrastination. *It's time to man up*—and then you just take action without hesitation. That's why these five words have been my mantra, a personal call to action, a war cry, and an instant reminder that it's time to do the right thing. Not the easy thing. But the right thing. In other words, it's time to do the work, right now, and do it all the way until I have the outcome I want to achieve.

As I followed this mantra after that fateful day, I cleaned up my diet and got back into regular exercise—embarrassing to admit since I'm a personal trainer at heart and fitness and health is my business. I went from mismanaging a hodgepodge staff to building a team of highly motivated workers who are driven to execute my vision. I went from choosing TV time over much-needed sleep to going to bed and rising at the same time each morning without hitting the snooze button. I went from living in a state of chronic anxiety—constantly anticipating future pain—to living with peace of mind, certainty, and definitiveness of purpose.

This book is the story of that transformation. I pull no punches on myself: You'll see, as you already have, me at my very worst, making stupid and costly mistakes that almost caused me to lose my home, shut down my business, and give up on my life's purpose. I'll share how I went from a stressed-out and overwhelmed failure to building a multimillion dollar–generating empire. I'll talk about how I went from nearly dying because of anxiety to having the chance to lead my business to success and investing in half a dozen other industry-leading companies in just three and a half years.

I wrote this book because I'm not the only one who has struggled like this, and I don't want anyone to have to go through the entrepreneurial anxiety attacks, financial struggles, depression, and self-doubt that I did. My success is also no accident—and this book is the encapsulation of all the suffering I hope you never have to go through to achieve your own. I want to help mold and influence the next generation of great leaders and entrepreneurs and show you how to stop making excuses, take control of your situation, and rise to your potential.

THE ONLY THREE THINGS THAT MATTER

This book will give you six pillars of effective entrepreneurial leadership, which can be distilled down to the only three factors you need to go from struggling to success—and to turn a good business idea into an industry-transforming empire.

1) You will become a self-disciplined (pillar one) and more effective leader who is able to communicate clearly (pillar two), make fast decisions (pillar three), and respond with certainty rather than react emotionally (pillar four).

2) You'll have a clear and defined vision for your business and a clear-cut path to help you get there (pillar five).

3) You'll know how to build your high-performance team: a hard-working, loyal, and driven group of employees who are committed to seeing your vision come true (pillar six).

This book is about you, the leader, your vision, and your high-performance team. Those three factors determine everything else. A lot of books focus on things like networking or marketing strategies or managing time. They miss the big things in favor of the small things. Not this book: We're going to work on the things that matter most, and I guarantee you the small things will take care of themselves, just like they did for my business.

Of the three elements, the first one is the foundation, which is why we start with it. How you lead your life affects how you lead your business. Maybe you stay up late, hit the snooze button, and try to duck under the covers. Maybe you've put your health and fitness on the back burner, and your body *and* your brain are suffering because of it. Maybe you're quick to blame others for your problems: the economy, the government, the competition, your employees, and even your clients and customers. Anyone but you. You do anything xxiv / Introduction: Being a Bad Leader Can Kill You (Literally)

to avoid looking in the mirror to take responsibility for where you are in life and business right now.

Everything changes when you man up. You go from wasting time on a daily basis to taking measurable steps and massive action on your destined path to success. You go from being an amateur to a pro, from a poser to the real deal. Whether you're a seasoned entrepreneur who is going through a rough patch, or a newcomer who is trying to figure out your way in the entrepreneurial world, or someone who just needs a kick in the ass for a change, this is the book that will finally help you break out of mediocrity, get singularly focused, and dominate in business—and in life.

Let's go.

Leading Yourself

L EADER ISN'T A TITLE. It's not a nameplate. It's not a set of awards. It damn sure is not your LinkedIn profile! Leadership isn't a what—it's a how. Leadership is being a visionary, a clear communicator; it's being decisive, staying in control of your emotions, and leading your organization from the front to victory with the least amount of stress, chaos, and lost revenue—and in the shortest time possible.

It's easy to prefer titles to outcomes. Yes, you're the founder, boss, or CEO. But does that make you a leader? Not if your business is falling apart or getting pummeled by the competition. Not if your personal life, relationships with those who matter, and your health are a train wreck. Not if you feel like there's a vise grip around your neck every single day.

It's time to step into real leadership—the kind that builds empires, leads high-performing teams, and turns ideas into industry game changers. In this section, you'll discover what it takes to lead your business to its fullest potential and, more important, how to become the effective leader that your business and employees so badly need.

CHAPTER ONE

Wisdom from an Unemployable Dropout

THERE WAS A TIME when I was not qualified to write this book. After all, I'm a foreigner from a Communist country. (Fun fact: My father was actually a member of the *real* Communist Party.) I was born in Armenia, a tiny country on what used to be the southernmost part of the Soviet Union. I could have very well been assigned a job working as a grocery store clerk, cab driver, or a car mechanic somewhere in Armenia had we not escaped the Communist Soviet Union in June of 1980.

My father bribed a Soviet government official with 25,000 rubles, which had taken him more than five years to save up, and my family (consisting of my father, Krikor, forty-six; mother, Suzy, forty-two; sister, Julie, twenty-two; brother, Sarkis, twenty; and me, the six-year-old baby of the family) escaped to Italy. Once there we went to the American consulate, declared ourselves as anticommunist political refugees, and asked for permission to come to the United States.

Permission was granted, and our lives would never be the same. My dad had $184 and we, a family of five, could only bring two suitcases. We arrived in America on June 15, 1980, landing at JFK Airport in New York. I remember thinking the whole airport was a city! It was a bigger and crazier swarm of people than I'd ever seen in the villages back home. We had nowhere to stay, so we spent the

3

night in the airport. My dad hadn't slept for days, but he stayed up that night to watch over all of us and our things.

The next day we flew to California, landing at LAX. My dad had a friend of a friend in Southern California. He agreed to pick us up and drove us to the nearby city of Cypress. My family sat in the back of his van, and I looked out the window and all I could see were lights and cars and wide roads. We were all dumbfounded and in awe—and that was seeing it in the dark! It was a forty-five-minute drive, and even in that short a time, we knew it was a big country. Certainly bigger than where we had come from.

We were given a spare bedroom in this man's apartment. All five of us lived in that one room for a month, like we'd come through Ellis Island in the 1900s and moved into a tenement. The morning after we arrived, this "uncle" lined up a paper delivery route for my dad that paid him ten dollars a night. At 2 a.m., my dad would leave us, get in the same van, and start throwing papers onto front steps. By day three, he got a second job as an attendant at a gas station. By the end of the week, he got a third job as a dishwasher at a pizzeria. The following week, my brother got a job at the same gas station where my dad worked. In one of the scariest moments during that early difficult time, my brother was robbed at gunpoint. He came home in shock. A couple weeks later, someone else tried to rob my brother at gunpoint again. My brother, for some reason I'll never understand, tried to grab the gun. The guy shot a few rounds that barely missed my brother, a near-death experience that would stay with him his whole life. Welcome to America.

My sister, who was now washing dishes at the pizzeria where my dad worked, came home upset one night. She told my dad about how the restaurant owner would take a sip out of her cup, just to make sure she was drinking water and not Sprite, because he wanted to make sure she wasn't stealing. Needless to say, she was grossed out that this guy sipped out of her cup every damn day. She was being paid less than minimum wage under the table. She couldn't say a thing to him. We needed the money, so she had no other choice. I remember when I overheard that my sister was unhappy with her job, I promised myself that one day I'd make so much money that she'd never have to work for someone like that again. Today she works for me, from home, on her laptop doing customer support.

I was only six years old, but I can remember that times were tough: We were broke, didn't speak the language, didn't understand the culture, and didn't know how we were going to make it. My brother and sister would come home crying every single day because they didn't belong, missed their friends, and wanted to go back to Armenia. We were yelled at and harassed on a regular basis, called every bad name in the book, and told, "Go back to your own fucking country, you fucking foreigner." That was how I learned the F-word.

My father wondered if he had made the right decision for his family. He had a sense that things would get better. He knew that we were in a wonderful country that offered us freedom and the opportunity to make something of ourselves—but first we had to overcome being poor and foreign.

Sometimes you can take a look at someone's later success and assume that they had a cushy life or an easy journey. Let me be clear: I've eaten out of dumpsters because at times we had no money for food. I've worn clothes we found in the trash that were more than a generation old and a couple sizes too small. I've had my hair washed with gasoline when my parents couldn't afford lice treatment. Wherever the bottom is, go a few feet deeper, and that's where my family and I started.

I never did well in school. I entered the public school system a few short months after landing in America, starting my school career before learning a lick of English. I remember literally pissing my pants because I didn't know how to let the teacher know that I needed to use the restroom. As if being the weird foreign kid wasn't bad enough, now the kids had another reason to pick on me. Being at school was pure torture. It was hell.

A couple of weeks into the school year, I started taking matters into my own hands: Instead of putting up with the ridicule and confusion, I ran away from the classroom. I'd escape and then bolt back down the street toward the apartment where my family was staying. The school would call my mom, who would start running from the apartment toward the school, and the principal would run after me from the school. I'd end up trapped between the two of them. Finally, my mom would drag me back to school, where I'd sit and imagine how to plot a better escape the next day.

One day, finding myself once again trapped between the worried principal and my upset mom, I found a piece of broken beer bottle on the sidewalk. Picking it up and holding it against my arm, I told my mother, in Armenian, that if either of them took another step toward me I would cut myself. Two adults, in a standoff with a suicidal six-year-old. It ended fine. My mom talked me down and I eventually put the glass down. I suppose this was my way of dealing with the stress of being a new kid from a foreign country and not being able to communicate or relate to the other kids.

My school career wasn't off to a promising start. After the incident with the broken beer bottle, the school found an Armenian translator to sit beside me in class, filling me in on what in the heck everyone was talking about. School became more bearable at that point, though it didn't improve beyond that: I've always had a bad association with anything school-related. Even today, a simple ad for back-to-school supplies gives me a stomachache and a mild sense of anxiety.

Part of that is that school was, for me, a source of instability. We moved around so much in the eighties that I never really had much time in any one school. I went to three elementary schools, two middle schools, and two high schools. My grades were awful, but as so often happens in the education system, the administration and the teachers just didn't want to deal with me, so they kept passing me along to the next grade just to get me out of their hair.

One high school teacher did try to talk sense into me one time. Her name was Mrs. Boyd, my eleventh-grade science teacher. By that point I had all but given up on high school, so rather than paying attention to the lessons in class, I'd sit by the door, look out at the school quad, and try to get the attention of anyone who was within earshot of my voice. Mrs. Boyd wouldn't have it. She'd storm up to me, yell at me to stand up, grab me by my shirt collar, and bang me against the wall with each word that came out of her mouth: *You . . . need . . . to . . . go . . . into . . . the . . . military! They're . . . the . . . only . . .*

ones . . . who . . . can . . . set . . . you . . . straight! In all her anger I don't think she realized that there was a fire extinguisher hanging on the wall right behind my head. Or maybe she did.

After high school I took her advice and went to the Marine Corps recruiters station in Anaheim, California. They said I had flat feet and couldn't join the military. So a year after high school I went to Fullerton Junior College to see if higher education was any different. I hated every minute of it and dropped out after only thirty-one days. Just like the other schools before it, I felt lost, confused, and out of place. I never even read books back then. If you told me I'd be writing one someday, I'd have laughed at you.

FROM FAILING AT BUSINESS TO WORKING AT DISNEYLAND

It wasn't just school: As proud as I am of my business successes today, I failed at my first two business ventures. I was never afraid of hard work. In fact, I got my first job at the age of thirteen at a local mom-and-pop grocery store. I emptied boxes of produce from their truck, rotated the produce in the walk-in fridge, and made sure the shelves were stocked with produce, cans, jars, and stuff like that. In high school I got a job at a bagel café.

I used all the money I earned from these jobs to start businesses back then. I guess you can say that I started young. My first attempt was a DJ business. When I was eighteen, I bought two very expensive turntables, a mixer, some speakers, and an amp. I loved hip-hop and dance music, and I figured I could make money as a DJ. Let's just say that business failed: The only event I ever DJ-ed, I did for free.

In that time, I also worked as a personal trainer. It wasn't a business success by any means, but I did train a handful of clients and I really enjoyed it. In the beginning, I had no idea how to make my personal training business successful. I had the right instincts about business, but I had no way to turn those instincts into results. Here's a good example: The year was 1997, and the internet was just coming around at this time. Websites that sold things were popping up left and right. I thought the internet was a great place to make money, so I launched my site totalmuscle.com. It was an online supplement store. I found out where the local supplement stores got their supplements from and I went and bought my own at wholesale cost.

I spent $55,000 I had saved up from my personal training gig and by charging up my credit card. I stored all the supplements in my tiny apartment. I figured the low overhead, the wholesale price, and my hard work would lead to riches. I hustled. I sent two to three hundred emails late into the night, every night, to prospective buyers. Not enough people bought from me to move the product fast enough, so the products expired and I had to throw them out. The $55,000 evaporated. I had maxed out my credit card, and because I used my rent money to continue to pay for the business, I got kicked out of my apartment. I needed to eat, so I ate what was left of the protein powder and protein bars. It sure beat eating out of dumpsters again. But I was constipated and sick all the time from eating all those protein products that I didn't want to toss out.

This was the beginning of my entrepreneurial career: catastrophic failure and constipation. It was a dark time. So after failing at school and failing at business, I found myself working at a big-box gym as a personal trainer just to make ends meet. But as anyone who has worked as a personal trainer in a big-box gym can tell you, the pay isn't great. So I had a side hustle as a bouncer at a gay bar. The gay bar paid more than the straight bars because skinheads would try to come into the bar a couple times a week to gay bash. It was our job as bouncers to make sure that skinheads never made it into the bar. I suppose the extra money was considered hazard pay. But even with the extra pay from the gay bar and the income from personal training, I still wasn't making ends meet. So I took on a third job at Disneyland. I worked as a busboy at Carnation Café, on Main Street, U.S.A.

I think everyone should work as a table busser at one point in their lives. Here's what I did as a busboy at the Carnation Café: cleared tables; washed dishes, glasses, pots, and pans; mopped floors; and deep-cleaned the kitchen every night, after the park closed, till 2 a.m. Every busboy hated the job. We'd return home physically exhausted and smelling of food. Plus, you got zero respect from the rest of the restaurant staff, who looked down on busboys.

But I paid my dues, and before long, I was asked to unpack pallets of foods that were delivered every morning. This was just as exhausting as busing tables, but I got to work normal hours and no longer returned home smelling of ketchup, mustard, and greasy hamburgers at two o'clock in the morning. Then I was asked to become a fry cook, then a dinner cook, and finally after five years, I was trained as a chef and got to wear chef whites and a fancy chef hat. (By the way, fun fact about the folds you see in a chef hat: There are one hundred of them and they signify the hundred ways to prepare an egg.)

I learned a lot from that time at Disneyland—but the best lesson of all was seeing firsthand the difference between a great leader who was respected by the team and one who was mediocre and earned no respect. This was a lesson that would be central to my future success. The lesson of poor leadership came in the form of a sour-faced manager—let's call her Kathy. As one of two shift managers who oversaw all the Main Street restaurants, Kathy had to make sure that the kitchen maintained standards and met a laundry list of rules and regulations set forth by the health department and Disney. Kathy would drop in randomly, usually at the busiest times in the kitchen, to stick thermometers in meats, inspect the ice trays, and look for any aspect of the kitchen that wasn't up to code. Yes, her work was important, but no one particularly liked the intrusion or the way she would disregard the kitchen staff during the busiest of times without ever giving a word of encouragement.

Kathy was one of those managers who didn't give praise, validation, or approval. It appeared that she only cared to point out shortcomings and mistakes we made. Add to that her pessimistic attitude, passive-aggressive way of communicating, and skeptical demeanor, and you've got someone who simply rubbed everyone the wrong way.

One busy day while manning the hot grill, I felt a pencil pressed against the side of my face, just under my left sideburn. It was Kathy. She noticed that my sideburns were a smidge below my earlobe, thus breaking the Disney dress code for facial hair. Kathy insisted that I immediately resolve this issue by making the trek to the employee locker room to find a razor and trim my sideburns up a quarter of an inch.

Never mind that no guests would ever see my sideburns back at the grill in the kitchen. Never mind that it was our busiest hour at the restaurant, with swarms of people in right before a parade was scheduled to go down Main Street. Never mind the fact that that very same parade would trap me on the other side of Main Street, keeping me away from the kitchen for a full forty minutes. The rest of the kitchen staff suffered without my help during that busy hour because Kathy had prioritized the length of my sideburns over the service and efficiency of the kitchen during a critical time. She failed to see the big picture, which was to keep the kitchen efficient and to deliver the Disney magic to the guests. Because of this, morale suffered and she lost the respect of her team.

The whole incident really bothered me. Sure, I was absolutely at fault for violating the Disney grooming standards. I deserved to be written up and even docked pay while I shaved back my sideburns. But all that could have happened after the parade passed and the restaurant went from chaos to manageable.

Kathy's counterpart, the other shift manager—let's call him Doug—was a tall, heavyset man in his late forties with a slight southern accent. Everyone seemed to adore Doug. During those busy times in the restaurant, Doug would come into the kitchen, flip his tie over his shoulder, and say, "What can I help with, boys?" Make no mistake about it, Doug was firm, did his job well, and maintained the restaurant and its staff to high standards. But he was also quick to give you a pat on the back for a job well done.

One thing I noticed about Doug was that he held the staff and restaurant to higher standards than even Kathy did, but everyone seemed to want to work harder for Doug. We didn't want to disappoint him. When Doug was our shift manager and the restaurant was packed, we'd skip our break in order to keep the kitchen efficient and the magic alive for the restaurant guests. We knew that when things got hectic in the restaurant, Doug would jump into whatever position was needed and work alongside the kitchen staff, servers, or bussers—and he did it with enthusiasm. That was my first experience with great leadership.

In a way, however, I have to thank Kathy for showing me what a poor and ineffective leader looked like. From that experience I realized I was never meant to be an employee. I learned that I wasn't made to take illogical orders from a leader whom I didn't respect. I could deal with it only as long as I needed to, and then I had to find another way.

There was one other thing I learned while working at Disneyland—workflow. I recall first getting into the flow during the two hours before and after the Main Street Electrical Parade, which made the Carnation Café literally the busiest restaurant in the entire country on any given night. Tens of thousands of people would line Main Street to watch the parade and hundreds of them would line up to come into the restaurant to eat in the outdoor dining area and to watch the parade.

When I was a busboy, we had to swoop in and clean off the tables, take everything back and wash them, and then bus the plates, glasses, and silverware from the counter and wash the pots and pans for the kitchen crew to use. To make the job more fun, I decided to turn it into a challenge in my head. I'd race to see how many tables I could clear with one bus tub, how fast I could mop the kitchen floors, or how high I could stack the racks of glasses and carry them out to the soda fountain. I'd pile glasses into one another and make a stack of ten or twelve of them in my tub to save room. I figured out a way to hold the bus tub above my shoulder with one hand so that I could wipe the tables down without having to go back to the kitchen to put the tub down. I was the most efficient busboy in human history, and in time, I found myself actually kind of enjoying the whole thing.

By the time my break and lunch passed and my shift ended, I didn't know where the time had gone. Back then I had no idea that I was in "flow" or what it meant. I'd just turned an otherwise stressful and low-paying job into a game—and I loved it.

On the surface, you wouldn't think this was the kind of job *anyone* could love. The servers would chew you out if a group left their table and you weren't swooping in like a hawk to bus that table so that they could seat a new family and earn more tips. The kitchen crew kept the stress on us, too. The cooks in the kitchen constantly yelled at busboys to bring them clean plates, pots, and pans. No matter how fast you worked, you could never satisfy the cooks, and they made it known. As a side note, when I got promoted into the kitchen, I, too, gave the busboys a hard time and rode them relentlessly. It was a rite of passage and we all loved the process.

When you turn something unpleasant into a game, you'd be surprised how far it can take you. Even though I was being yelled at and my body was exhausted, my clothes were a mess, and my hair reeked of food, I felt like every day was a challenge and I enjoyed that. I wanted to beat the total number of tables I could bus in an hour. Or I wanted to do it faster. Or I wanted to find a way to cut some step out of the process and make my job more efficient.

I didn't know about the science of flow then. I didn't know that research actually reveals that you can get into a state in which your mind and body are in unison, in which the hours just fly by. I just knew I had experienced something amazing and I wanted to experience it again—only this time, I'd be the boss.

BACK TO BUSINESS

After seven years of working at Disneyland, I had saved up some money and I quit. I went into personal training full-time, which I felt was my purpose.

This time was different—because I had a mentor. One of my clients was an older gentleman named Jim Franco. We'd train three times a week. He was in his early sixties and was a self-made millionaire who had started an automotive software business and grew it into a multimillion-dollar company. If you walked into a mom-and-pop auto parts store and the guy behind the counter typed in a specific car part into his computer, it was Jim's company, Autologue, that provided and updated the software for him. Until Jim, those auto parts stores operated out of paper manuals. After Jim, they had computers, which made them faster and more efficient.

Right away, you could tell from his poise and self-confidence that he was someone to learn from. The moment he walked into a room, people took notice. The gym would light up when Jim came in. The ladies loved him, and even the guys in the gym would smile wide when he looked their way. He could develop rapport with anyone, and so fast that you didn't even know he was charming you. He had a personal magnetism and confidence that I thought was powerful, and that I knew was one of the secrets behind his business success.

He had enormous personal discipline, but he also brought joy to his work and his office. He would arrive early every morning and greet every single employee with a smile. I was invited to his office Christmas party one year—and it was actually fun. A lot of times those events feel forced; you can tell that people don't want to be there, and they are only doing it to make sure the boss takes notice. Not at Jim's office. Everyone had a blast, and Jim dressed as Santa Claus. He personally handed each employee a bonus check and thanked them for their work. You could see in people's faces that they were happy to work for Jim. For me, he set the bar for what office leadership looked like. Later I would think back to Jim and his office morale and culture so that I could replicate it at my headquarters.

As I trained Jim, I would pick his brain about the art of entrepreneurship. He was rough around the edges, cocky, and confident—but he was also a shrewd businessman. I would watch him and learn so much just listening to his stories about business. Disney had taught me that I was unemployable and couldn't work for anyone else; I needed to learn from Jim how exactly to work for myself without going broke. As I pushed him through his workout, he taught me everything he knew about running a business. It was like getting an MBA—but being paid for it! He liked me, too, and came to believe in me, eventually loaning me $126,000 to start my own business. I paid him back with interest over time, but the fact that he took that big of a gamble on his personal trainer was a real vote of confidence for me.

After Jim's mentoring, I had gained enough confidence to start my own personal training studio. That personal training business grew big and profitable until I sold it. After the sale of that business, I went on to coaching and consulting in the fitness industry for the next half decade, and I'm happy to report that my clients and I had great success. But just like my personal training studio, it wasn't a scalable business. It was a glorified job. If I stopped working, it wouldn't keep working. I was ready for more. I wanted to be more than just "self-employed."

Learning how to become more than just self-employed took a long time, but it led me to where I am now: the CEO of Fit Body Boot Camp—one of the fastest growing franchises on the planet, with nearly a thousand locations worldwide. But its roots started small: an immigrant kid who basically faked his way through school, failed at some businesses, and worked as a busboy at Disneyland. To give you another sense of just how small those roots were: When I was a personal trainer, my immigrant father would tell people I was a masseuse. He didn't understand why anyone would pay someone else to train them in the gym. "They paid the gym membership," he'd say in a thick Armenian accent. "Why don't they just lift the weights and use the machines?" I tried explaining to him that I got paid to help people with their health just like a massage therapist does. So I was a "masseuse" to him from that day forward.

It's become common these days to talk about entrepreneurs once they've achieved their successes. We put them on the cover of magazines; we give them awards; we put them on television. People are a lot less comfortable talking about the long journey to those successes. They don't want to talk about the crappy jobs they've had; they don't want to talk about the awful bosses they had to deal with. But the story of those valleys is what makes the story of the peaks worth it.

EXERCISES

At the end of every chapter, I'm going to ask you to do some exercises. You can write down your answers and thoughts if you want. Or you can just spend some time thinking about them. Don't flake out on these. They matter—a lot. Manning up isn't a light switch that flips. It's more like a dimmer switch that slowly glides from where you are now to where you need to be. It's a process that develops over time and a big part of that process is reflecting, processing, and strategizing. It's thinking hard about your life, your past, and your decisions and future desires. No one said this was going to be easy—and if you're really eager to man up, you don't want it to be.

So here are three sets of questions I'd like you to think about before going to the next chapter:

1) All great entrepreneurs have great mentors. They have people they study and look up to. Who is the person in your life that you're studying and learning from?

2) I discovered flow state by washing dishes and cleaning tables. But now, it's a state I try to cultivate in everything I do. When do you experience flow? When does the time fly by for you?

3) Not being good at school was important for me. If I had been good at school, I probably wouldn't have become an entrepreneur. All of us have something like this: something that seems terrible in the moment that ends up being a transformational fork in the road guiding us to some of our greatest successes. Can you identify something in your life like that? Something that has served as a transformational fork in the road for you?

CHAPTER TWO

Getting Your Shit Straight

FOR ME, manning up didn't happen overnight. The process that started in the doctor's office took a long time. And it wasn't just a process of doing specific things. It was a way of changing how I thought about things—including killing off a lot of negativity and damaging belief systems in my head that were holding me back.

That negativity had childhood sources. My family came to this country with nothing. And my dad would say, over and over again, "We'll run out of money before we run out of month." That became my mind-set: We'll never have enough. Life was a series of tough choices: Do we pay for the water bill or gas bill this month? Do we buy a used car or try to find a better apartment that's not in a gang-infested area? A nice dinner for us, even after several years in the country, was eating at Sizzler. We needed a really good reason to go out to eat. There was a lot of negativity in the house because of our financial situation. My dad didn't mean to be negative or pessimistic, of course, but it was hard not to be gruff when we were penny-pinching that way.

As a kid, because of my family's circumstances, I became obsessed with finding the cheapest way to do things. I told myself a few stories that quickly became the narrative of my life: (1) that I was a foreigner, and foreigners don't make it; (2) that I'd always trade my time for money; (3) that I was blue collar and I'd stay blue collar; and (4) that I was a bad student, would always be one, and bad students don't become successful. All of it led to poor self-esteem, poor self-image, and a lot of negative self-talk.

I had to fix this. One of the things that my mentor Jim Franco did was give me a sales cassette tape to listen to. He prefaced it by telling me I was terrible at selling (which got me angry) and then told me the tape would help (which got me interested). That tape led to other self-improvement tapes, books, and programs, and before you knew it, I was devouring the genre. If you name it, I read it, listened to it, or went through the course. Tony Robbins. Jim Rohn. Maxwell Maltz, Dale Carnegie, Napoleon Hill, Les Brown, Brian Tracy, Zig Ziglar, Dan Kennedy. All of them. At one point, I remember standing in the corner of the gym and jumping up and down yelling, "I like myself! I like myself! I like myself!" Sure, I felt a bit foolish, but I also knew that I had decades of negative self-talk in my head that operated like a virus, and I had to throw every cure I could find at it. I had just learned about the power of incantations from a Brian Tracy book and I used it several times a day. Still do. There wasn't any one thing that helped me—it was the whole batch of exercises that helped to turn the negative self-talk and limiting belief systems into positive self-talk, beliefs, and habits.

I even went into intense therapy after my massive anxiety attack. For almost three years my therapist helped me work through a lot of issues from my childhood. Things that had led to depression and anxiety had roots in my childhood, and it wasn't enough to just try to mask over them with success. What I had to do was get at the source of the problems, to do so with a professional, and to deal with them. I tell you this not to say that you necessarily need therapy, but because a lot of the stories in our lives that control our self-image and self-esteem have old and deep origins that can't be ignored until you process through them. Listen, here's what I know to be true: We look at the world through the filters that we have on. Those filters have been shaped by your experiences from childhood on up. If you think that trauma, no matter the form—mental abuse, physical abuse, or sexual abuse—is something that you can simply "manage" and overcome without doing some serious deep work, then you're in for a big surprise.

This is a big part of manning up: getting rid of self-limiting beliefs through a process I call "releasing the emergency brake." When I first started to do the work on myself, I had to wrestle with the fact that a lot of what was in my head were negative statements about who I was:

- ▸ I wasn't smart enough because I hadn't done well in school.
- ▸ I was a bad provider because we seemed to always be on the edge of bankruptcy.
- ▸ I was never going to succeed at business because I hadn't succeeded in the past.
- ▸ I was not a good leader or manager of people because I was introverted.

Until you take control of self-limiting beliefs, they will manifest in many different areas in your life. For example, you might have a negative money mind-set that your parents put in your head. Perhaps they told you that money's bad, money's for the rich, that other people have success and we don't, that we're the working class and will never be anything else, or that the rich have knowledge or opportunities that you simply don't have access to. I guarantee you it affects your business. That negative belief system is crippling. After all, your beliefs dictate your habits, your habits dictate your actions, and your actions dictate your outcomes.

The negative self-talk in your head and your heart that's been there for so long has got to change. Our childhood experiences shape us—and they shackle us. You might know the feeling. There are other pains from the past that can keep us in a mental prison. You might have been on the receiving end of a cruel comment from a school-teacher, family member, or other kids. Or maybe you got regular beatings from your dad, or maybe you were sexually abused, or had addicts for parents. All these things lead to trauma that when not processed and dealt with can limit your personal and professional success, happiness, and growth the same way a sports car can be neutered in performance when it's driven with the emergency brake slightly engaged. Because of my trauma, I found a million reasons in my life to fail at things, sabotage my success, and reduce the impact I was making. Looking back, I failed at things on purpose. Procrastination was one of my bad habits ten years ago before I released the emergency brake. I'd have a good idea and set it aside for "the future," and then never get around to it.

All of these were stories—narratives I had sold myself on. And I had to shed them to reduce the mental friction in my life. It's no different than when you lower the e-brake on your car and all of a sudden it performs the way it was designed to perform. You're clearing out the clutter in your mind so you can make room for beliefs, habits, and actions that will help you and not hold you back. You're going to do that, at long last, by releasing the emergency brakes that have been holding you back.

EMERGENCY BRAKE #1: FEAR

I have witnessed fear and self-limiting beliefs stunt the success of more of my coaching clients than any other factor, just as I've experienced the grip of fear in my own life.

In 2005, I applied to speak at the National Strength and Conditioning Association conference and the IDEA Fitness conference. I wanted to speak not about personal training but about the *business* of personal training. There are lots of people who can get you fit; I knew how to take that whole operation and turn it into a profitable business. I was politely rejected from both.

It made me mad to get rejected—so I decided to create my own event: The Fitness Business Summit. My wife and I built it together. I basically assumed there were a lot of people out there like me who had the personal training part down, but needed improvement in client management, marketing, and business management. It was a good idea, until we saw the sticker price for hosting an event like that. It was enormous. Our personal circumstances didn't help matters. Di was pregnant with our second child. We had just moved into a new home. We didn't have the resources we have now.

But we decided to go for it. Come February, we had a conference— with fewer than half the attendees we expected and less than half of what we expected to charge. I wasn't an authority in the industry yet, so that made sense. But at the time, it made me freak out. Add to that my biggest fear of all: public speaking. I hate it. It terrifies me. Every night for two months before the conference, I took NyQuil to go to sleep because I had crippling fears about speaking at the conference. I feared for my reputation. I worried people would laugh at me, that they would hate the event, that the fitness industry would shun me, and that I would be broke.

I was awash in fear. But guess what? The event wasn't the success of my wildest dreams, but they didn't banish me from the industry because of it, either. We barely made it work financially, but we did it. The fears I had were utterly out of proportion to the possible negatives.

What I've learned over a lifetime of similar experiences is that fear and insecurity guarantee failure. If you're looking left as you're driving a car, you'll pull the steering wheel left, even if you don't mean to. Same goes with fear and insecurity. If you're fearful, you'll give in to those fears. That's why FDR's line rings as true now as it did when he said it at the height of the Great Depression: "The only thing we have to fear is fear itself." We should be afraid of fear, because it will hold us back.

It might be that you're afraid of criticism, afraid of what other people might say, afraid of what your family might think or how they'll judge you, afraid of failure, and even afraid of success.

Instead of going all out and being the high-performing human you're meant to be, you hold back because you're being selfish and protecting yourself from what others think.

When it really comes down to it, the only thing you legitimately have to fear is the possibility that you'll allow fear to prevent you from taking the necessary action required to reach your life goals. You will have to think hard about what you're afraid of and then design a plan to deal with it. This won't be easy, and honestly, you might do what I did for so long: avoid dealing with these fears.

But on the other side of that work is freedom. It's the freedom to do what you were actually meant to do. The freedom to walk around without the weight of the world on your shoulders. The freedom to enjoy your success and push through your failures—without feeling like everything is going to collapse around you.

EMERGENCY BRAKE #2: POOR MANAGEMENT OF TIME AND ENERGY

Before I manned up, I was the master of procrastination. All my early businesses—the DJ business, the supplement company, the personal training—all of them suffered because I would put things off. Fear led me to waste time and energy by putting things off. I would choose going to the beach over preparing for the next day's work. I'd stay up late and watch television and then wake up late and hit the snooze button. I had horrible work habits.

I did a lot of busywork. A good example: One minute, I'd have an idea. And I'd use that one idea to pull me away from working on the others. I'd flit from thought to thought, business to business, all the while not getting any single big thing done. I'd tell myself that I was "working on my business," but I wasn't. I never went far enough down the road on a specific task to execute on anything meaningful. I was stalling. I wasted all kinds of time, money, and opportunity. And I blamed everything but my poor time and energy management.

Listen, if you play the blame game and claim to be too busy and overwhelmed to get what you want out of life, then slap yourself silly. That's an amateur belief system and it's not serving you well. It's an outright lie that you tell yourself—and the people around you.

It all boils down to time, energy, and priority management. You make time for the things that are important. What's important to you? The truth is that right now, it's very likely that the things that you are prioritizing over doing your life's work are downright embarrassing. The time and energy you spend on recreational "fun" activities, screen-sucking social media, useless emails and text messages, and binge watching TV shows, or taking unscheduled calls and meetings, are killing your business. They're killing you!

Managing your energy, your sleep, and your health is just about as important as it gets. It's the foundation for everything else in your life, and I'm telling you as someone who nearly died because of anxiety that if you don't take care of your body, it won't take care of you.

EMERGENCY BRAKE #3: ASSESSING YOUR TEAM

Nick was an amazing hire for Fit Body Boot Camp. He practiced jujitsu, he worked hard, and he was always happy. He knew how to coach our FBBC owners and how to get things done. Nick came in with a lot of good raw material. Unfortunately, he also saw, when he came into the business, that a lot of people around him didn't have his discipline, enthusiasm, and work ethic.

I didn't lead him well, not at all. It was a huge failure on my part. Over a three-year period, he fell into a funk. I blamed him. Only later did I learn that it was because of what I was doing—or more accurately, *not doing*. I wasn't leading him. But he had the potential to be led and to become a really critical part of my business. It's a real shame that he quit. (To his credit, he went on to start his own business.)

It was a real wake-up call for me when Nick left. Here was someone who could have helped me and my business grow. He could have worked up to a position of leadership and great pay, but he left because of my failure of leadership. I vowed never to let that happen again.

Fast-forward to 2013. A woman named Joan walked into my office. I could sense she was a killer. She was Nick-like—she had poise, self-assurance, and that instinct. This time, I wasn't going to fail as a leader.

Up until that point, I had been doing a bad job of taking care of myself. From 2007 to about 2012, I lost my discipline. Even though I was a personal trainer, I stopped working out. I was stressed-out all the time. I started eating fast food. Predictably, I put on a lot of weight and lost my hard-earned muscles. I took NyQuil and Vicodin to go to sleep; otherwise my constant state of overwhelm would keep me up all night. But in hiring Joan, I knew those bad habits weren't going to cut it: I couldn't risk losing her due to things I could fix myself.

It took a lot of work. It took a lot of time in the gym and cleaning up my diet. It took a lot of clarifying my vision, figuring out the path, and telling myself over and over that it was time to man up. But a big part of what motivated me was the people in my life—my wife, my kids, and my team, including employees like Joan. Once I realized I was manning up for them—and not just for me—it became easier to stay accountable and get things done.

Often when people talk about their team, they talk about their employees. But I want you to think about your "team" broadly: Think about the people in your life. What do they add to your life? What do they subtract? Do they bring positivity, energy, and strength? Or do they suck your soul with complaints, excuses, and nonsense?

When you hire employees, are you genuinely excited about them or do you bring them aboard because you need to fill seats? Extend this to your friendships and personal relationships. How deliberate are you about the people in your life? We're going to dive much more deeply into this later in the book, but it's important to think about this as one of the emergency brakes in your life potentially holding you back.

These aren't easy questions. But you need to ask them. You need to do a thorough assessment of the people you've let into your company and your life. And remember: *You've* let them in, so it's on you to be honest about what they are doing in your life.

EXERCISES

1) Open up a document on your computer or take out a piece of paper. Divide it into four columns:

The Fear	The Outcome	The Likelihood	What Can I Do to Prevent It?

You may not get this all down in one sitting, but I want you to be brutally honest with yourself and write these things down:

- FEAR: What are you afraid of right now that's stopping you from getting what you want? What's the feeling in the pit of your stomach?
- OUTCOME: What happens if what you're afraid of actually occurs? Be specific and detailed. Be gory. Give yourself permission to outline it in all its awfulness.
- LIKELIHOOD: How likely is it that what you're afraid of will happen? You can estimate in probabilities or you just can make a statement like, "It may happen sometime before December."
- WHAT CAN I DO TO PREVENT IT: This is where the rubber meets the road. Write down the tactical steps you're going to take to prevent the outcome from happening. One way I do this is by going outside of myself by saying: How would I advise a friend if they approached me with this issue? I don't care if the plans are tangible or pie-in-the-sky; write down every strategy or tactic you can think of.

2) Open up your calendar from the last two weeks and make a list of the people you spent time with. If you didn't schedule the time, then write down their names. Stop when and if you get to ten people. (If you run a company, do this with your employees and partners, too.) Now stop. Take a look at those ten people and go name by name. Ask yourself these two questions: Are these people adding value to my life or business? Are they taking value and costing me time that can be better invested in others?

3) Sit down and write out three BIG things that *must* get done on a daily basis in order to keep your momentum up. Now refuse to waste a single minute doing nonessential time killers before these three are completed. Wake up in the morning and tackle these three things first. What should you choose? Let me offer some suggestions:

- Meditating
- Morning workout

- ▸ Reading for twenty minutes
- ▸ Journaling ideas to exponentially improve your business or life
- ▸ Sending a gratitude email or text message to three people you value
- ▸ Improving one system in your business that will increase profits, service, or reach
- ▸ Executing at least one thing every morning that will move the money needle

The truth is you can find what you need to keep your energy up. This process is about writing those things down and committing to them.

CHAPTER THREE

The Nonnegotiables: The Only Secret . . . Is That There's No F-ing Secret

I T SEEMS THAT everyone today wants a hack. They want a get-rich-quick scheme. They want a silver bullet. They want the code. They want the right stock. They want the pill. They want the one thing they should do to become rich, famous, beautiful, successful, and happy. Guess what? The hack doesn't work. The scheme will fail. The silver bullet doesn't exist. The code won't get you through the door. The stock isn't there. And the pill . . . well, any pill promising that much is something you ought to stay away from.

You'd be surprised just how many people believe that there is a grand *secret* that the successful use to get to the top, and that once they learn this secret their lives will improve. Here's the secret: There is no secret. There is no shortcut. There is no hidden door. Do you want to know how the most successful in life get to the top of any given industry? They know, understand, and live by the following four nonnegotiables.

NONNEGOTIABLE #1: WORK ETHIC

At the office, I stay focused and work on the things that matter—things that make us money, improve our products, service, and client experience, and things that secure future growth and scale. I make sure that my team knows that I'm willing to do anything they are. During crunch times, I arrive early, stay late, and am always prepared. No excuses. I've learned, over time, the difference between working hard and working smart. Overworking on the wrong things, getting overwhelmed, and having poor communication were what led to my anxiety attack. I work hard today, but I work smart—on the things that matter. I don't get overwhelmed because I have a strong team that I can delegate tasks to. Plus, I have healthy habits and clarity of purpose that keep me from having another anxiety attack. If opportunities come to me and they're not aligned with my vision and purpose, I take a pass. I used to be the guy who never passed up an opportunity—the guy who tried to work hard on everything. Today, I say NO to most things so that I can say YES to the things that matter the most to me and work hard on them.

Working hard is just the ante at the table. If you are allergic to hard work, you can kiss your purpose good-bye. What is hard work? Hard work starts with having clarity of what you want to accomplish—clarity of your outcome. Remember, hard work isn't impressive if it's poorly managed and it wastes time. After all, you only get paid for what you've done. When you have clarity of your outcome, the hard work starts each night by creating a list of things that you are going to attack the following morning. Hard work is waking up early every day to make the time to focus on one thing uninterrupted and with discipline until completion. The work must have purpose so that you're not throwing yourself against a brick wall or running in place; it means doing the important thing and doing it well. That one thing may be reviewing your tax liability, filming a sales video, spending an hour writing your book, or calling twenty influential people to network with and move your idea forward.

Hard work is, above all, hard. That sounds like I'm just repeating myself, but I'm not. At the end of a good session of hard work, just like the end of a workout, you should sit back and say, "Holy shit! That was difficult. I'm drained. I'm thrilled, but I'm drained." There is a big difference between shallow work and what the author Cal Newport calls "deep work." Deep work is hard work. And it should tax you, make you think, make you sweat. It's a state of focused concentration that not only requires your best, but also brings out your best.

Many people think that they are working hard and they are getting shit done when they are really doing meaningless, easy work. This busywork manifests itself as research, as perusing social media, checking emails, and being unstructured and undisciplined with time and activities. It's easy. It feels good. And it's useless.

NONNEGOTIABLE #2: NO EXCUSES— PLAY LIKE A CHAMPION

During my teenage years, I was fat and out of shape. I was first motivated to work out and get fit so I could have enough confidence to ask a girl out to the senior prom. Even though I was motivated, I started riding an excuse carousel: "I don't know how to eat right and exercise, so I may as well keep eating the terrible stuff I've been eating." Never did make it to prom. The same thing happened later in my career. I thought I should start a franchise, but I didn't know how, so I used the excuse of not knowing how as a way to let myself off the hook.

I could find excuses with the best of them. My business is failing? It's because I'm a foreigner. My networking isn't as good as it could be? It's because I'm putting in all this time to provide for my family. My heath is failing? It's because I can't afford to work on that when I have to work so hard in my business. I had a doctorate in making excuses. In order to man up, I had to learn that excuses were hollow armor. That they were a reflection of bigger issues and deeper problems—a poor self-image, low self-esteem, and limiting belief systems I had formed from childhood that were holding me back. Then I had to fix them.

Has that little voice in your head piped up yet, telling you that all of this sounds great, and good for you, but that none of it will work for you because of X, Y, and Z? The excuses have arrived, my friend, just as to be expected. You're not alone. Nearly everyone who has ever done anything big first had to wade through the bullshit excuses that popped up in their head. Know this: Excuses kill dreams and plant the seeds of future regrets. The key is to push through the excuses, and to not let them slow you down, impede your progress, or take you off your path of greatness.

When you examine them, excuses are simply insecurities and fear of the unknown. You may be *saying* that the market is too saturated for your product, but what you are *feeling* is that what you have to offer simply isn't good enough for the market to want. Design a better product, be a more-valued product or service for the marketplace, hone your craft, get obsessed with service and support, and squash your insecurities with rock solid confidence.

Excuses give us false comfort. *I would have achieved my dreams, but since X, Y, and Z happened to me, I simply couldn't.* That's an easier narrative to swallow than the truth: *I simply didn't want to put in the hard work and face the challenges that stood between me and my dreams, so I didn't even try.* Make no mistake about it, an excuse may feel comforting in the moment, but at the end of the day, or when you lay on your deathbed, you will only feel the pain of regret.

Excuses are a lot like sugar: They taste good in the moment, but they are damaging over the long haul. That feeling will fade. The sugar high will crash. That's how excuses work. Banish them from your life. Elite performers leave no room for excuses. They own up to everything and take control of the situation.

NONNEGOTIABLE #3: ADD VALUE CONSTANTLY

One of the biggest lessons I learned from my father was to add value all the time. Even when he first stepped foot onto U.S. soil, his thought was, "How do I add value?" He wasn't thinking about it in an abstract, touchy-feely way: He knew that adding value was the way to get paid. That's what a job is, after all. So that's what he did. He took a paper route. This was a job that teenagers did. But he knew that, in that moment, it was the easiest way to add value and thus get paid. His subsequent jobs—pumping gas, for example—were the same thing. He found the quickest path between where he was and where he could add value, and then he got paid.

Even though he got paid very little, my father gave me a lesson that has always stayed with me. I'm always asking myself, "What can I do to add value to this person, situation, business, or problem?" It's like a filter for the rest of your life: In every context, you can add value, and when you add value, you get paid. You can be stuck in a business that's going nowhere and you can think about how to add value. You can be in a job you utterly hate and think about how to add value and fall back in love with your job.

Will you be a value extractor or a value adder? Every day you have the opportunity to choose one of those two attitudes. I look at it like this: Each morning we can put on one of two shirts. Shirt one says, "What can you do for me?" Shirt two says, "What can I do for you?" The universe rewards value adders—people who come with a giving hand, without expecting anything in return. The best evidence I have for this is my own success: The more value I've added to people's lives, the more I've gotten in return.

I think this is also connected to the difference between people who have scarcity mind-sets and those who have abundance mind-sets. The scarcity minded watch what everyone else is doing in fear instead of focusing on creating value and solving problems in their business. They are jealous. They blame outside circumstances—their parents, genetics, the economy, lack of education, poor timing, the competition, you name it—for their lack of success, lack of happiness, and impact. They blame others while refusing to take personal responsibility. Scarcity-minded people falsely assume that others have greater control over their success than they themselves have.

The abundance-minded individual believes that there's more than enough for everyone and that the more value you add, the more you'll get in return. They are not selfish. They genuinely get a high, a happiness, from helping others and seeing people achieve and accomplish whatever they set out to accomplish. Abundance-minded people help, connect, truly care, and demonstrate their care through actions, not just words. Their motivation for adding value is not gain, but oftentimes, the outcome is that they get more than they expected back. That's just how the universe works; it rewards value adders and takes away from value extractors.

Add value to others and you'll get back value to yourself. It's that simple. It's what the best in the world know intuitively; it's what you need to drill into yourself until it's automatic.

NONNEGOTIABLE #4: CHOOSE TO BE A FIGHTER JET

I'm going to be somewhat politically incorrect here. This world is divided into two types of people, crop dusters and fighter jets—and it's not evenly divided at all. The majority, the crop dusters, are folks who are complainers, approval seekers; they're indecisive, and unorganized in their thoughts and actions. Crop dusters are drifters, wandering through life without purpose, passion, or a sense of urgency. This is not to say they don't have *any* purpose or don't feel a twinge of guilt or urgency from time to time when they are hit with the reality that time is passing them by. But the pain isn't great enough for them to take action and command control of their lives—*yet*.

Crop dusters don't think ahead; they seldom have the desire to do something greater than themselves, and they're satisfied with just making enough money to get by. Crop dusters aren't meaning-, impact-, or service-driven. By nature, crop dusters are a selfish bunch and think of themselves because they are always operating out of a sense of entitlement and often see themselves as victims. What I mean is that they're always in debt, live paycheck to paycheck, lack a sense of purpose in their lives, and are allergic to hard work and commitment . . . but they blame others and their circumstances and never seem to take responsibility for where they are in life. In that way, crop dusters make for horrible entrepreneurs, leaders, and employees.

Crop dusters seem to live to be average. They do just enough to pay the bills and keep their heads above water, but even that is only temporary. Sooner or later life throws them a curveball, as it does with all of us, but crop dusters find themselves unprepared—that's when things really get bad for them. Crop dusters choose the easy, short road of immediate gratification over the hard, long road of a lifetime of meaning, money, and security. I know this because I was a crop duster. I was the guy that chose easy over hard. I blamed everyone and everything for my circumstances but me. I didn't consider myself "average," but everything about me *was* average—even though I had extraordinary potential. I suffered every day. Average people suffer because they're always one or two paychecks from going broke. Security doesn't exist when you're average. You can't help the causes and charities of your choice when you're average, because you simply don't have the money to make the impact that you want. I remember feeling that way.

Looking back, I don't understand why I chose to be average. Or why I was okay with the idea of mediocrity. Maybe it's because I didn't see myself as mediocre or average. I just saw myself like everyone else around me and that made being average acceptable. But I'd never tell my kids to get average grades, to think average thoughts, to grow up and get an average job, have an average marriage, be of average health, and live an average life. Thank God that I came to my senses by feeling the pain of being average and by having mentors in my life who had higher expectations of me and showed me that I have excellence within me and that it's my duty and obligation to reach my potential of excellence.

So How Did Being Average Become Okay?

At some point we begin to accept average and mediocrity as the baseline. If you ask, most kids will tell you that they want to be a doctor or a veterinarian, a firefighter or an astronaut. This is because kids are born with aspirations and no limits on their ability to dream. It's not until they acquire years of experience and observations of friends, family members, and authority figures that a glass ceiling begins to form over their heads, and their expectations of what they can achieve in life begin to drop and harden.

Who said that just because you're doing better or equal to the competition that it's good enough? Why don't you work harder and smarter and put your competition out of business? Then you'd really solidify your long-term success and security. Who said it's okay to ignore your inborn potential and instead use the mediocre people around you as your barometer for success?

We are all to blame. We have raised generations of kids who are rewarded for mediocrity. *You participated but didn't win? Good job, here's an award anyway.* By doing so, we've been conditioned that average is good enough and we've carried that into our work ethic, our health, our finances, and our relationships, and this has lowered our expectations of ourselves and the expectations we have of others. What a shame.

If your business is capable—and the market space is available—of making $100 million per year, then why are you okay with making $2 million a year? If you and your spouse are just two ships passing in the night, without depth or meaningful conversation, why are you okay with that? Living as strangers is as good as divorce. If you're only ten, fifteen, or twenty pounds overweight, what made that okay? Because everyone else is? Get down to your fighting weight—your health, business, and family depend on you.

It is your destiny and it is your duty to your family to create security. It's your responsibility to provide a better life for your kids than you had.

It's time to expect more from yourself. Raise the bar. Don't be a crop duster. Raise your standards. Dream bigger. Aim higher and expect more of others.

The Fighter Jet

We both know that you're not reading this book because you want to stay average. You're a fucking fighter jet! The simple fact that you chose to start your own business and be an entrepreneur tells me that you are a fighter jet. You see, crop dusters may get an entrepreneurial itch from time to time, but it's usually when their boss yells at them or when the "idea fairy" stops by with a good idea—which they'll likely never take action on.

You simply don't have that luxury to be or act like a crop duster if you've chosen to be an entrepreneur. You can't go to bed late. You can't sleep in and hit the snooze button. You can't be indecisive. You can't be undisciplined with your health, exercise program, mind-set, nutrition, time management, or productivity.

Entrepreneurs are fighter jets and fighter jets are high-performance. You simply cannot be lazy, unstructured, or indecisive if you plan on being a successful entrepreneur. You've chosen to be a risk taker, a creator, and a problem solver, and that tells me that you're a fighter jet. The thing is, perhaps no one has ever told you that you're a fighter, let alone how you should operate as a fighter jet. No one has ever encouraged you to strive for your fighter jet potential or to listen to your instincts.

Most of society looks down on fighter jets. You're also known as a black sheep or they might have described you as "having your head in the clouds." Odds are your parents haven't instilled fast decision-making in you. On the contrary, they've raised you to play it safe, be a team player, and do as the rest of the flock does. They've encouraged you to get a formal college education, to get out and find a good secure job, and to work hard and hopefully work your way up and retire from that company.

Do you know what happens when fighter jets are raised by crop dusters?

Do you know what happens when fighter jets are educated by crop dusters?

Do you know what happens when fighter jets hang out with crop duster friends?

They begin to think and act like a crop duster, even though they have fighter jet ambitions and instincts. It's like taking a lion who's meant to hunt and rule the African Serengeti and putting him in a cage in a zoo and feeding him meat regularly. Sure the lion will live, but it will lose everything about it that makes it the king of the jungle. There is no faster way to kill the spirit of a lion than to put it in a cage, feed it meat a couple times a day, and stop it from hunting.

According to *Forbes* magazine, 13 percent of Americans are entrepreneurs—but that alone doesn't make them fighter jets in my book. We also know that 80 percent of businesses fail, or at best, simply flutter along, sporadically breaking even but mostly causing stress and anxiety in the lives of the poor bastards who started them. So it's safe to say that many entrepreneurs start as fighter jets but become crop dusters when they underestimate the amount of time, money, and effort that is required to get their business off the ground. I was one of them.

You see, crop duster entrepreneurs assume that going into business is going to be easy. They think, "If I build it, they will come."

The reality is that you built it and no one came. No one cares about your better mousetrap. No one cares about your better service and how you're revolutionizing an industry. No one's out there waiting for you to create the better business model. Fighter jet entrepreneurs know these facts. And once I understood this and accepted that fact, then everything changed for me!

Fighter jet entrepreneurs build a better mousetrap, and then they commit to doing the necessary work to out-market, out-sell, and out-service the competition. They find creative ways to use influencers to get the word out about their products or services. They're always finding better and faster ways to leverage social media sites, search engines, apps, and video sites to spread their messages. Fighter jet entrepreneurs commit to becoming effective leaders. They're decisive, they're great communicators, and they have clarity of vision. They focus on personal growth and development as much as they focus on business growth. They work at becoming emotionally resilient. While crop dusters are emotionally reactive, fighter jets have mastered the art of managing their emotions. Rather than emotionally reacting to a situation or problem, which causes people to lose respect for them, fighter jets respond with calmness, focus, and strategy to situations, which further solidifies their leadership and authority. Fighter jet entrepreneurs also understand the value of building a strong team of effective employees who are driven, loyal, and capable of bringing their vision to fruition.

As I said, most entrepreneurs start off crop duster minded. They overestimate what they can achieve in one year and underestimate what they can achieve in five to ten years of disciplined and focused work. They underestimate how hard it will be and how much work it will require. They hire employees who have the skills but lack the drive and ambition. Skills can be taught—passion, drive, high self-motivation, and a fire in the belly cannot.

But everyone has the ability to become a fighter jet. It's not like being a fighter jet is reserved for some special people. This book is written with the intent to help you become the fighter jet that you so badly need to be. Fighter jets are the type of entrepreneurs we look at and say, "Now there's a natural leader!" They are the people who seem to be an overnight success. They make growing an empire look easy. They have clarity of vision and clarity of path where their business is concerned—more on these key elements in the next section.

Fighter jets are experts at self-mastery. They have control over their emotions, thoughts, and actions. Fighter jets rarely react emotionally; rather, they respond deliberately and with calculated precision. They take extreme ownership of everything in every way. They're respected by their peers, loved by their employees, and recognized throughout their industry. They're decisive, highly focused, and outcome driven. Their self-discipline goes beyond business. They exercise regularly, they don't sacrifice sleep for entertainment, they're sharp as a tack, they eat to live rather than live to eat, and they invest time in personal growth and development. While most people think that fighter jets are naturally great leaders, I can tell you with 100 percent certainty that most were not born a "natural" leader—they've simply developed great leadership skills by doing the work.

Be honest with yourself: Are you a fighter jet or a crop duster entrepreneur right now? Let me tell you something that no one else will tell you: Many of the most successful entrepreneurs today, those who we consider great leaders, started off just like you. But to become successful and to reach their fullest potential, they made the decision to man up—and that made all the difference.

The Six Pillars of Effective Entrepreneurial Leadership

PILLAR #1: SELF-DISCIPLINE

If you can't lead yourself, then you can't lead a team.

Self-discipline is needed in each of the following three categories:

1. **Your body:** Keep your body lean and conditioned. Eat right, exercise hard, and get enough sleep. This is the difference between being energetic and unstoppable versus being sluggish and sick. It's a big deal! Having self-discipline with your body impacts virtually every aspect of your life and business. Let your body go to shit and watch how quickly your growth is neutered in business and in your personal life.

2. **Your mind:** Only allow positive influences into your mind. Start by turning off the news and surrounding yourself with uplifting people. Make no mistake about it, keeping your mind free of negative influences takes concentrated, disciplined effort. There's nothing wrong with censoring much of the world around you in order to feed your mind the positivity that it needs to thrive. Be ruthless in screening negativity out of your life. Your thoughts control your actions, and your actions control your outcomes.

3. **Your time:** As an entrepreneur, your days are often unpredictable, and you don't have the tightest schedule. This creates a slippery slope toward chaos. It's vital that you hold yourself to a disciplined schedule. Do this by creating your attack list the night before. Your attack list is made of the three to five things that you are going to accomplish in your business that day. Go to sleep at the same time each night and wake up at the same time each morning, then get started right away on your attack list. Nothing else happens until your attack list is complete. This is how you control your morning in order to control your day.

> ## How Self-Discipline Serves You
>
> As an entrepreneur you aren't like a regular human. There are higher demands on you. Very much like a high-performance sports car, you must take better care of yourself in order to be fully operational. Your level of self-discipline carries over into every aspect of your business and team. Through self-discipline you're able to function at your highest level.

EXERCISES

1) Find a Work Ethic Model

The very best performers in the world all have models for excellence. Kobe Bryant studied Bruce Lee. Franklin Roosevelt studied Teddy Roosevelt. Elon Musk studied Nikola Tesla. Part of why they do this is because we can learn about the habits and techniques that make great people great—and then use them ourselves. After all, success leaves clues.

I can tell you who I look up to where personal discipline and work ethic are concerned: Craig Ballantyne. I call him "the most disciplined man in the world." He's the one who got me to understand the value of getting up early; he's the one I credit for a lot of my personal discipline, structure, and morning rituals that led to my business success. But what I admire most about him is his work ethic.

I want you to find your role model for work ethic. Good role models get things done; they get the right things done. They are that person who everyone goes to when something needs to be completed. They execute.

Find someone you know who is a no-bullshit hard worker, someone you resonate with, and ask that person to mentor you. If you want, you can imagine that you're interviewing this person for a podcast. Talk about the books this person reads, the routines and rituals this person follows, and the habits that make this person's life tick. There's two reasons to do this: (1) You may learn some things that you can adapt to your own life, and (2) work ethic is contagious.

It rubs off. Hardworking teams produce hardworking people. You want to be around and be talking to people who work insanely hard.

2) Keep an Excuse Rubber Band

This one's easy: For a few days, wear a rubber band on your wrist. When you make an excuse, snap it and let the pain set in. It's that simple. This'll rid your life of excuses. When you make an excuse, just snap the rubber band and tell yourself: It's time to man up—and then do so by immediately taking action to create the outcome that you want.

3) How can I evolve into a fighter jet?

What fighter jet characteristics are missing from your life? List them. What crop duster habits and belief systems do you have right now? List them. Every week pick one crop duster habit or belief system and replace it with a new fighter jet characteristic.

CHAPTER FOUR

Fix the Leaks

B Y 2013, the reality had set in: I knew in my bones that I wasn't a good leader. For years, I blamed everyone and everything when things went wrong, but I now realized that I was the one fucking it all up. Like most business owners, I thought I was a good leader, but the reality was that I was a very poor and ineffective one. When I first started Fit Body Boot Camp it was just me, my business partner, and one employee. There weren't a lot of moving parts or people to keep track of. The pace was slower, more manageable, and we all did our part the best we could. But as the business grew and got more complicated, and as we hired more employees, I felt the pain and pressure of leadership. Rather than stepping into it and learning how to lead a team to success, I did the exact opposite of what an effective leader should do—I avoided responsibility and chose not to grow as a leader as my business grew. Instead, I showed up late to meetings. I was always unprepared. I didn't correct, mentor, or give feedback to my employees who needed it. I avoided the conversations that I deemed uncomfortable. I pretended that everything was under control. I assumed that everyone would self-manage and get their work done. I kept my feelings bottled up until they turned to resentment. Resentment turned to adversarial relationships. And that led to a toxic work environment where everyone walked on eggshells and no one felt safe to voice their concerns.

A good example: By early 2013, I knew my business was struggling and that I had lost control of my employees and the direction that Fit Body Boot Camp was headed, so I hired a consulting company to help us. They were supposed to help create systems for my new franchise business. We were paying them $22,000 a month for their help—money that we did not have available and went into debt to obtain. This was my Hail Mary to save the company, and I was willing to go further into debt if it was going to save us.

The consultants were good guys and tried to do the best they could. They came in very motivated. The problem was that I kept pulling them into everything that wasn't their core focus. They were supposed to fix our systems and operations, but I asked them to help with everything from sales to marketing to traffic generation. Essentially, I tried to turn them into a proxy CEO—the leader I wasn't!—and it's because I wasn't willing to look hard in the mirror and own the business. Part of me assumed that they could do it better than me. I quickly learned that there's really no white knight who's going to gallop in and save your business. You're it. I was it and I refused to accept it.

Soon, the consultants started slacking off because I had put so much on their plate that was outside of their "zone of genius," and since I wasn't asking for or tracking results they simply started to lower their efforts to match mine. They were supposed to be at our office a set number of hours on a set number of days. That started to fall apart quickly. They made excuses. I accepted them. We were paying them enough that they wanted to keep the contract, but I had led them badly and I had spoiled their chances to help me. In hindsight, I can't blame them for slacking off. I blame myself for not giving them clarity or key performance metrics to strive for. They got just as complacent as the other employees we had. This was all a by-product of poor leadership on my part and nothing else.

See, that's the thing: When you get good people but put them in an environment with low standards, few expectations, and poor leadership, they begin to slip. I saw that first with Nick and now

I was seeing it with these consultants. And since we were paying them more than $20,000 a month, it was too painful for me to avoid. My mantra came back to me: It's time to man up, Bedros. It's time to man up and part ways with these guys or you're going to go out of business. So I gave them their thirty-day notice and took matters into my own hands. It wasn't as easy as that—untangling the relationship was a pain for everyone involved, but I had to do it. I had set a bad precedent as a leader and now I had to fix it or go out of business and file bankruptcy.

You can't outsource leadership. I tried. I've seen others try. You are the leader and, like it or not, you're running your company. You're either going to guide them to greatness by taking ownership, rising to the opportunity, and becoming an effective leader—or you're going to take your business into the shitter like I did by doing nothing, ignoring and avoiding your role and responsibility, and attempting to hand off leadership to someone else.

Since then I've had a lot of time to think about bad leadership, try to develop into a capable leader, and study models of success. For me, a big part of fixing my leadership issues began when I was able to diagnose why I was weak and ineffective. I took notes; I talked to people around me; I went to masterminds; I attended seminars and read books on the topic. And I came up with what I now know are the Seven Deadly Sins of Weak and Ineffective Leaders.

1) **Poor communication:** One clear sign of ineffective leadership is poor communication. Leaders who are unable to clearly share their vision and communicate problems, solutions, and recognition effectively tend to have high employee turnover, low morale in the workplace, and poor culture.

2) **Lack of action and follow-through:** Leaders who do not have a bias toward action and follow-through are among the most ineffective. They expect others to do the work, make the decisions, and call the shots while they stay isolated and inactive. Indecision (lack of action) has cost entrepreneurs more money, time, and market share than making the wrong decision or taking the wrong actions.

3) **Disconnection:** Keeping isolated or disconnected from your team, business partners, clients, and customers is a sure way to erode respect, loyalty, and confidence in your leadership.

4) **Weak character and integrity:** Leaders who lack character and integrity will never have trust or likability by those who work for them or by those with whom they do business.

5) **A negative perception of others:** Ineffective leaders tend to find fault with most people and focus on the things that have gone wrong. They often seem irritated and have a negative perception of team members, the industry, and their customers.

6) **Lack of vision:** One telltale sign of weak leadership is a lack of vision for the business. Ineffective leaders fly by the seat of their pants and are reactive in the way they do business, thereby creating a sense of confusion, chaos, and instability.

7) **Poor personal discipline and structure:** Ineffective leaders lack personal structure, so they often chose the path of *easy* in their personal lives rather than choosing the hard work that produces results. They have chaotic schedules, are disorganized, and always seem to operate in a state of overwhelm and irritation. Weak leaders lack the discipline to structure their days, their thoughts, and their actions, and they constantly have their priorities out of order.

I started with the negatives, in part because, at one time or another, I've committed all these sins. (Oscar Wilde once said, "The only difference between the saint and the sinner is that every saint has a past, and every sinner has a future." He's right!) I've been disorganized and a poor communicator. I've been indecisive and lacked vision, and so on. But it's important to identify these deficits before you can correct them. You've got to take honest stock of the places you're falling down, and then you can figure out how to work to pick yourself back up in those areas. Sometimes, it takes someone else identifying those spots for you.

SEEING THE WEAK SPOTS

One of my coaching clients, Byron, is a very enthusiastic, driven individual. A simple conversation with him fires you up so much that you want to join Team Byron. His enthusiasm is contagious. Early on, Byron owned two Fit Body Boot Camp franchise locations in Arizona. He had amazing potential to grow his empire. Even though he had the potential and desire to own many more FBBC gyms, for some reason there was a limiting factor that kept Byron from reaching his fullest potential—and I was about to discover exactly what it was.

It wasn't until Byron joined my mastermind program that I got a better understanding of the things that were limiting him. I run several mastermind groups for entrepreneurs and each of them meet three times a year for two days at a time. The goal is to help, guide, and direct each member through their business challenges and bottlenecks while finding hidden growth opportunities. Any group of like-minded entrepreneurs can start a mastermind together with the intention of helping one another achieve greater success and holding one another accountable.

During the mastermind meeting, Byron seemed on top of it. He was doing all the right things in his business, with his marketing, and with sales. Yet the numbers on his profit and loss report didn't show it. His attrition rate (the rate that a business loses clients or customers) was through the roof. If it wasn't for his lead generation and online marketing strategies, his business would be losing clients faster than it was gaining them. Another red flag I noticed was that his clients didn't do a lot of referring. In a business such as personal training, or any high-end service for that matter, one of your strongest marketing systems should be advocacy, or how often clients recommend you to other people. But this wasn't the case for Byron. A lack of referrals is usually an indicator that something is wrong in the business.

During the lunch break, I asked him to sit with me because I could tell that he wasn't giving us the full picture of his business during the mastermind session. We got to talking about his business, and he mentioned that his employees weren't on the same page as he was. This was clearly causing him a lot of frustration. He went on to say that several of his employees had so much potential, but until they stepped it up and did a better job he wouldn't be able to open up more Fit Body Boot Camp locations.

That was my first clue that he didn't have an employee problem (people rarely do). He had a leadership problem. Employees should never be the limiting factor. I asked him what might have seemed, in that moment, like an odd question: "Byron, what's your morning routine?" He went on to tell me that on some days he'd wake up at around six thirty and other days he'd wake up at seven or seven thirty.

I then asked him what his top two or three tasks were first thing in the morning. He responded with, "Well, that depends on if there are any fires to put out." Naturally, I asked him what kind of fires he was talking about. He replied, "Well, if my trainer missed the first workout session of the morning then we might have twenty or twenty-five pissed-off clients. So I have to deal with that sometimes."

"Okay," I said. "Tell me what time you normally go to bed."

"That depends," he said. "Some nights I'll be in bed by midnight. Other times I'll be up and working on my business till two in the morning." Burning the midnight oil, as I said, is usually not a good sign. He was working hard but not smart.

"Tell me about your eating habits," I said. Byron went on to explain that he tried to eat healthy for the most part, but many times he would be starving during work hours only to come home and binge on a big dinner, a few glasses of wine to take the edge off, and something sweet before going to bed. He was stress eating, operating out of the fight-or-flight state. I suspected he was depressed and that he probably didn't know it. And this guy was training other people to be healthy!

"Tell me about your workout habits," I said.

"Oh, yeah," Byron said, "I need to get back to working out regularly again. I just have so much going on right now that I don't have time to work out regularly. To be totally honest, I don't even have the energy." It was as plain as day to me: Byron was burned out and overwhelmed.

This is the point in the conversation when I said, "Byron, can I be brutally honest with you for a moment?"

"Sure, of course!" he said.

"Byron, you're a bad leader. You have great qualities, but right now you're not living up to them. You're a hypocrite." It was the same conversation I had with myself that fateful afternoon when I left the doctor's office after experiencing that massive anxiety attack a few years earlier.

I told him about the two patterns I noticed—and I noticed them because I had been guilty of some of these same things myself.

Pattern 1: His use of "Yes, but . . ." followed by a reason why something that he intended to get done hadn't worked out. You know those people who use "um" too much in their speech? Byron had a similar verbal tic: "Yes, but . . ."—and it was indicative of a much bigger problem. He was hooked on excuses: "*Yes*, I'm not eating well, *but* it's because I'm working too much"; "*Yes*, I'm not able to get the business on track, *but* it's because . . ." And on and on. Pointing this out was the first step to helping him break the habit.

Pattern 2: The man didn't match the message. There's a great line from Ralph Waldo Emerson: "Who you are speaks so loudly I can't hear what you say." It's something I think all leaders should ponder. In Byron's case, he was struggling personally, and he had bad habits. It affected his authority and his ability to lead people. He had all the right people in his organization, but he was incongruous with his message. If there's one thing I know, it's that you can shout about getting things done all you want, but people can take one look at you and know if they should follow you. Byron hadn't made himself followable. Hypocrisy is the fastest way to erode trust in your leadership abilities. The only way to lead is to lead from the front.

When you first hear someone tell you that you're a bad leader, it comes as a bit of a shock. But if you're growth minded and know how to put your ego in check, then it could be the start of something new and incredible. For Byron, that's exactly what it was—an opportunity to become a great leader so that he could build the business of his dreams. Over the next few weeks, Byron gave me open access into his personal and professional life. We started doing the work to make him an effective leader.

HONESTY ABOUT YOURSELF BEFORE ALL ELSE

I don't want you to have a distorted view of yourself, and believe me, you're the easiest person you can fool. It's just too easy to buy into your own hype. One of my favorite quotes on this comes from the Russian master Fyodor Dostoyevsky. He said, "Above all, don't lie to yourself. The man who lies to himself and listens to his own lie comes to a point that he cannot distinguish the truth within him, or around him, and so loses all respect for himself and for others. And having no respect he ceases to love."

I once read a study in which one hundred people were asked to rate themselves on intelligence, communication skills, decisiveness, and work ethic. Something like 92 percent of the people ranked themselves well above average in all areas. Later these same people were tested in all four areas, and, wouldn't you know it, almost the exact percentage who ranked themselves well above average actually ranked below average in all four areas.

So I'm asking you to be brutally honest and fully transparent with yourself. Or to find people who will be that honest with you. Feedback is the food of constant evolution and improvement. You need someone to point out when the emperor has no clothes. You need people in your life who will level with you about your leadership weaknesses, because that's the only way you'll get to work on them. Without feedback we don't get an objective view of who we are and therefore can't become who we need to be to reach our fullest potential.

That's what Byron did. Our conversation was a wake-up call. He spent the next two and a half years manning up. This started with a deep assessment of his self-esteem (how you feel about your self-worth) and his self-image (how you think others see you). Together, your self-esteem and self-image determine what level of success you will rise to; if you'll self-limit before reaching your potential; whether you will tolerate mediocrity; if you'll be approval seeking; how you will handle stress, criticism, and setbacks; and, most important, if you will give yourself permission to be worthy of success, achievement, recognition, and wealth.

For Byron, this meant he would have to rein in his personal life first: start eating better, go to bed earlier, get back to exercising regularly, and join the 5 a.m. club with me. Then he'd work on the deeper factors that influence self-esteem and self-image like shutting down his negative self-talk, overcoming his limiting belief systems, fixing his relationship with money, and setting higher expectations and standards for himself and others around him.

Just two and a half years after our talk, he opened up his fourth Fit Body Boot Camp location. Byron is proof that change in business, culture, and expectations start at the top. Your business, your team, and your income are simply a reflection of your leadership quality. His trainers and staff have turned up the dial on their "give a shit" factor, so, not surprisingly, his clients are getting better results. Because he takes pride in his business, so does his team. His clients love the workout community that Byron and his team have created. But before Byron could make any changes with his staff and within his business, he had to start with himself.

That's where you start, too.

The Six Pillars of Effective Entrepreneurial Leadership

PILLAR #2: CLEAR AND EFFECTIVE COMMUNICATION

Your communication skills (or lack thereof) influence every interaction that you have with your employees, customers, vendors, and business partners.

Most of us were raised to be polite, often making us apprehensive about clearly communicating how we feel, especially when it comes to expressing negative feedback. These neutered communication skills make it very difficult for anyone to know what you really want. When your team members don't get a clear message from you, they aren't able to produce the outcome that you're looking for. Miscommunication quickly breeds passive-aggressive behavior and sets an adversarial tone for your relationships, which leads to setbacks, frustrations, and lost potential.

The solution is to speak with absolute clarity, to be specific, and to ask that the person across from you repeat back to you what your expectations are so that there is no misunderstanding whatsoever.

How Clear and Effective Communication Serves You

It has been reported that poor communication in business leads to increased employee turnover, poor customer service, higher litigation costs, and stunted growth. In study after study, poor communication is cited as the number-one reason that businesses fail to move faster. Avoid this problem and experience fast growth and market domination by utilizing clear and effective communication.

EXERCISES

Leaders Take Responsibility

Think back to your last failure. I want you to rewrite the story of how it happened, only this time I want you to take full responsibility for everything that went wrong as you tell the story. Take every single moment and turn it back on yourself. Rewrite that narrative. Now take a look: What does that tell you about your leadership? How does it feel to have all the control in your hands?

Leaders Keep the Garbage Out

I don't check emails or texts, take calls, or surf social media in the mornings. Anyone who does is wasting time, and it's going to cost them dearly in the near future. The mornings are my time to GSD— Get Shit Done. This is when I work on my business and focus only on things that will move the needle. When I'm doing important work, I put my phone on silent mode, flip it over screen-side down, and push it more than arm's length away from me. This may sound excessive to you, but for me, it's all about protecting my "magic time" in the mornings and focusing on getting shit done. I don't want to be tempted by sounds or notifications on flashing screens, so I take every precaution to kill the temptation.

Disciplined leaders have guardrails like these in place all the time. When I have my computer open and I'm working, I have my emails closed, the volume on mute, and social media closed. I'm not here to build Mark Zuckerberg's business, I'm here to build mine.

Good leaders are careful about tilling their mental gardens. They are careful about the information, distractions, and noise they let into their lives. You need to do the same thing. So try the following:

1) Turn off the notifications on your phone for one day. I don't mean turn off your phone. Just the notifications. How did it feel? How did it go? How much more time did you have to focus on your stuff?

2) Install an app like RescueTime and do a quick scan of where your online time is spent. Where are you wasting precious hours? You'll be surprised to discover how much your device robs both your business of productivity and your family of meaningful time with you.

3) At the end of the day, look at your to-do list and your schedule. Did you get things done today? Did your time actually match up with the things you needed to get done? If not, what do you need to do to prevent time theft tomorrow?

CHAPTER FIVE

The Beginning Is the End: Fix Your Mornings

I HAD THE PRIVILEGE of working with Craig Ballantyne, an amazing entrepreneur, on his business. He helped me fix my life.

Craig is a successful businessman and author. He advises some of the top performers in the world about how to structure their days for maximum impact and outcome. But what's even more impressive is not where he is today, but where he started from. His dad was an alcoholic; his mom an enabler. He grew up wearing hand-me-down clothes. He grew up on a farm, and when he wasn't in school, a lot of his days were spent just sitting with his dad on a tractor as his dad drank and plowed the fields. Because of that, and a lot of other difficulties, Craig suffered from social insecurities, anxiety, and stress. He drank a lot. As he once told me, "Bedros, I had green eyes, a black heart, and a yellow belly." By his own admission, he was jealous, self-centered, and cowardly—likely traits that he adopted through environmental exposure to his father.

But if you met him today, you'd never guess it. Through a process of rigorous self-development and self-improvement, he's become a great communicator and one hell of a business mentor to many high achievers. It's why I sought him out—and he's one of the reasons I went through the transformation process that helped me evolve into a better leader. There was one morning I remember vividly: We were supposed to meet for a workout early and then attend a mastermind after the workout. I was going to have a late night so I texted him, "HEY MAN, I'M SORRY, NO WORKOUT TOMORROW MORNING. I HAVE TO CATCH UP ON WORK. I'LL MEET YOU AT THE MASTERMIND."

A lot of people might have texted back, "COOL MAN." But what makes Craig great is that he called me on my bullshit. "WHY DO YOU HAVE TO CATCH UP ON WORK SO LATE AT NIGHT?" he texted.

I didn't really have a good answer, but I tried: "WELL, I WOKE UP LATE AND JUST GOT JAMMED UP."

He didn't accept that, either. "DUDE, WHY NOT JUST WAKE UP EARLIER?"

"I'M NOT A MORNING PERSON," I replied.

Again, Craig could have accepted this answer, but he pushed me: "OKAY, TRY THIS: JUST GET UP A HALF HOUR EARLIER FOR A WEEK."

Honestly, at first, I didn't appreciate what he was doing. I didn't think I could squeeze a half hour into the day, and I definitely didn't want to cut a half hour out of my sleep. But then I thought about it, and it wasn't a huge ask. I could at least *try* it and if it didn't work out, I'd have an answer when Craig asked.

I tried it for a week. Honestly, it felt amazing. That extra half hour was real time. Since no one was awake, I was able to get a few extra things done and make my morning appointments without too much pressure. When I came back to Craig and told him about the first week, he said, "Great. Do another half hour earlier." I tried that, too. It was like I bought myself a free hour in the day. I kept doing this until I was up by 4:30 or 5 a.m. each day. It also forced me to shift my dinner and the rest of my life so that I could go to bed a lot earlier.

The early wake-up time enables me to build a morning ritual. It allows me to plan out my day, practice gratitude, and make sure my mind-set is in the right place. It gives me plenty of uninterrupted time to work on my list of big ideas. Here's the truth: Your morning ritual is everything. It's the anchor of your day. It tees up the rest of your day for success. Craig helped me do this in person, but I'd also recommend checking out his book *The Perfect Day Formula*. It goes into how to do this for yourself. Take it from someone whose life has been changed by organizing his mornings, the payoff is huge.

Consider professional boxers and MMA fighters who have very specific rituals that they go through before getting into the ring. They call this the Starting Ritual—and some of them can become astonishingly specific. For example, one heavyweight champion goes through eleven individual steps during the preparation for his fight. He always gets his left hand wrapped before his right. He plays the same song in his headphones repeatedly, and that song puts him into his "warrior state." He has the same three people in his prep room and no one else. He refuses to say a word between the time he gets his hands wrapped and the time he enters the ring. Instead, he repeatedly replays the visual of himself winning the fight in his head.

A starting ritual is a simple process that you do each morning to put you into a state of effective work. This is a form of mental preparation for battle. Over the last fifteen years, as I worked closely with countless entrepreneurs, I found that those who are the highest of performers have very specific morning routines. Those who have the most productive morning routines have a consistent starting ritual that gets them into the right state of mind for them to do their best work. You can look at it like the prelaunch checklist that NASA goes through before catapulting a rocket with astronauts in it into space. Every flick of a switch, every turn of a dial, every confirmation of a system brings them one step closer to a successful launch. This is what's missing in your life.

The act of going through a consistent morning routine does so many great things for you. It quiets your mind. It gets you mentally prepared to work. It gets you singularly focused on the task at hand that's going to produce the biggest positive shift in your business.

Here's what my morning ritual looks like:

▸ Even though I wake up at 5 a.m. every day, my morning routine starts the night before, about two hours before bed time. That's when I go to the notes section of my iPhone and write down the three to four high-priority things I'm going to attack the next morning when I sit down to work. My list is rarely longer than four things, and it's always in order of importance. In other words, my highest priority task is always number one on my list. I do it this way so that even if the day unexpectedly turns to shit, as it sometimes does for us entrepreneurs, at least I got the most important task done first thing in the morning.

▸ Once my alarm goes off at 5 a.m., I never hit the snooze button, because I believe when you hit snooze, even just once, you're telling your subconscious mind that you value ten more minutes of mediocre sleep over getting up and living your purpose. When you hit snooze first thing in the morning, you've already made your first conscious act of the day—and it was an act of weakness. I spring out of bed and I go right to the bathroom to clean up, shave, and shower. I want to be fully awake and alert when I go downstairs to drink my water, coffee, and protein shake.

▸ Your body dehydrates a lot throughout the night simply from breathing. Since your brain works best when it's hydrated, I found that drinking sixteen ounces of water first thing in the morning helps clear the mental fog and hydrates my body.

▸ After greeting my wife, Di, and letting Cookie, our eighty-five-pound mastiff mix, out to do her business, I get my laptop, sit on my favorite spot on the couch, and look at my list of three to four things I need to do that morning. Then I'm ready to attack it. Before I start to work, I put my phone on silent, turn it screen-side down, and push it away so I can attack my list without distraction. This one act keeps me focused and productive during my morning routine.

▸ I banish social media during this time. I don't check Facebook, I don't want to know what's happening on Instagram, I don't care what the president tweeted, and I'm not interested in who emailed and texted me overnight. I have my attack list to dominate. This focused chunk of three-hour work from 6 to 9 a.m. allows me to do the big things that move my business forward.

▸ By 9 a.m., I'm done with my list and spend the next forty-five minutes or so replying to emails, text messages, and posting on social media (not for fun, mind you, but for my business).

▸ By 10 a.m., I'm in my car heading to the gym to get my morning workout in for an hour or so before I head to the FBBC HQ to meet with my team leaders, create new content and courses, do podcast interviews, shoot videos, and arrange new business deals and growth opportunities.

I credit this morning routine for much of the transformation that took me from weak and undisciplined to focused and strong. There are other benefits, too, some of them unexpected: Because so much of the important work gets done before everything else invades the day, I don't end the day feeling guilty. I used to walk around feeling not just unproductive, but also ashamed at being unproductive. I'd come home, my mind elsewhere, and I'd tell myself I couldn't spend time with the family because I was busy. That was bullshit: I wasn't busy. I was just disorganized, and I didn't have a morning routine dialed in that let me get solid work done.

Once I fixed it, I not only didn't feel that guilt, but with the weight of it off my shoulders, I was able to spend time with my family that was fully about them. You will be shocked at the aftereffects of a simple fix to your morning routine. If you take one thing from this book, let it be that.

MORNINGS ARE A HABIT

Part of the reason the morning routine works is because it becomes a "keystone habit." That's a term that psychologists use to discuss the one habit that, if you change it, enables you to fix and repair a lot of the other things wrong in your life.

Back when I had my fateful felt-like-a-heart-attack anxiety attack, I tried to figure out the cause. I looked at my habits. At the time, I had cut my workout days and times in half to accommodate my business. I had allowed clients and customers to cross boundaries by making myself available to everyone morning, noon, night, and weekends via text, email, or phone. I had taken on businesses and business partners whose values did not align with mine. These were the bad habits that caused me to fall apart and slide into a depression.

After seeing how one small habit led to another small (and equally bad) habit, I made the decision to reverse each bad habit one by one for the sake of my sanity, health, family, and business. I started with my mornings—but once I fixed those, it became much easier to dial into everything else. Once I knew I had the power to shift my behavior and that a small shift could have such a big improvement, I went on figuring out what else I could change, like a world-class chess player who clearly sees his next four moves.

But it all started with fixing the mornings.

EXERCISE

This one's easy: Get up a half hour earlier. No tricks, no gimmicks, no writing anything down. Just figure out when you normally wake up, dial it back a half hour, and DO NOT HIT THE SNOOZE BUTTON when your alarm goes off. Try it for a week and see how it goes. If it goes well, then go back another half hour. It goes without saying that you can't rob yourself of sleeping time. So in order to wake up a half hour earlier, you will have to go to bed a half hour earlier.

CHAPTER SIX

The 5 Percent Rule

S EVERAL YEARS AGO, I learned a very painful and expensive lesson in only three minutes. In just 180 seconds, I lost $5,000—at a time when I couldn't afford to lose $5,000.

I had just started my coaching and consulting business. I had only one employee working for me and she was my assistant. Our office was the spare bedroom in my house. We had just sent out an email promotion to my list of email subscribers that offered them the opportunity to get a day of business coaching with me for $5,000. The email promotion went out at 8 a.m., and at 9:30 my wife came upstairs to let me know that one of the sprinklers in our backyard had sprung a leak and was shooting water everywhere.

Since I'm a pretty handy guy, I decided to fix the broken sprinkler myself, knowing it would take me only twenty to thirty minutes to fix. But just when I was elbow deep in mud and pipe glue, my assistant came to the backyard to tell me that she had a qualified lead who was interested in my $5,000, one-day coaching program. Since I was literally stuck in the mud, I told my assistant to close the deal herself. After all, she had heard me close deals like this one on several occasions and I felt that she could do it. Plus, I had a sprinkler to fix!

After fixing the broken sprinkler pipe, I washed off and went back upstairs. I found out that my assistant was unable to close the deal. I realized in that moment that making a broken sprinkler pipe a higher priority than my business cost me a $5,000 sale. I could have easily paid a lawn maintenance guy twenty-five dollars to fix the broken pipe.

Holy hell!

I chose to do trivial work that I should have delegated to someone else and asked my assistant to do the critical work. A $5,000 sale was lost because I was doing work that was outside of my "zone of genius." That wasn't good leadership on my part, and it certainly wasn't a good client experience that I delivered.

The 5 Percent Rule was born in that moment: I focus exclusively and unrelentingly on the 5 percent of things in my business, and life, that only I can do. It's simple: When you apply the 5 Percent Rule to your business, it will free you from the trivial tasks that waste your time, and it'll save you from doing things that are outside of your zone of genius, which you can pay someone else to do.

Just because you know how to fix a broken sprinkler pipe, change a light bulb, write payroll checks, or make a website doesn't mean that you should be the one doing it. Let's be honest, there's a lot that must happen to keep your business running, but most of it can be outsourced to others. Someone's got to do the marketing, selling, servicing, fulfillment, bookkeeping, account receivables, new product or service development, writing of payroll checks; someone's got to clean the restrooms, stock supplies, run profit and loss reports, do quarterly taxes, and all the things that need to get done just to keep the lights on.

But it doesn't mean that *you* should be doing these things. You see, of all the things that must be done to keep your business running, only 5 percent of them are the critical few that should be done by you, and these are the things that really move the income needle. Your 5 percent might be the calls that only you can make or meetings that only you can take or opportunities that only you can seize. The remaining 95 percent are the tasks that can be done by others, often for $25 per hour or less.

Why on earth would you do work that's trivial and that can be done by others for relatively low cost? I don't think you're going to see Richard Branson in the cockpit of the next Virgin Atlantic flight that you take. He doesn't fly the planes or serve you wine and peanuts (though there is that hilarious photo of him dressed up like a female flight attendant going around on the internet). He works on his business and focuses on the 5 percent of tasks that only he's capable of accomplishing to produce growth.

HOW DO YOU IDENTIFY YOUR 5 PERCENT?

For my client Byron, I had him make a list of everything that he does for his business in a one-month period. Then I asked him to put the letter *C*, for critical, next to all the high-value tasks that fall into his 5 percent. He then put a *T*, for trivial, next to all the other tasks that he could delegate to others. Remember: An effective leader spends his day working *on* his business and not *in* it. For that to happen you've got to identify the critical tasks that fall within your 5 percent and spend most of your day working on those things. Then find competent people and delegate the remaining 95 percent of the trivial tasks so that you never have to do them yourself.

YOUR TO-DO LIST AND YOUR NOT-TO-DO LIST

To be high-performance in your work, you've got to start your day with a to-do list. That said, your *not*-to-do list is just as important. Let me share a few of the many things on my not-to-do list:

1) I will not go to the grocery store.
2) I will not go to the dry cleaners.
3) I will not write a press release.
4) I will not write a blog post.
5) I will not book flights and hotels.
6) I will not answer my phone if someone randomly calls me.

Here's the best part: Just because I won't do it doesn't mean it won't get done. Thank God for my amazing team and my wonderful wife and family. They handle a lot of the tasks I listed above and dozens more so that I can focus on building the business to its fullest potential, which ultimately helps everyone! They do these tasks for me because I've made it clear what I am working on—the things that only I'm capable of doing.

Let's be clear about one thing: A not-to-do list isn't a not-*want*-to-do list. You can't put items on this list just because you want to avoid them. The point isn't to continue ducking the difficult. The point is to isolate the few things that you're uniquely suited to do and that drive your business forward. Manning up isn't about dodging things or skirting your duties. On the contrary, it's about stepping up to do the really hard things—and making sure you have the strength and bandwidth to do them right without feeling overwhelmed or rushed.

Your not-to-do list is there to protect your time and make sure that you're spending it on the highest value work—the work that delivers the best results in profits, service, and outcome. And in your personal life, your not-to-do list is there to ensure that you do not do the activities that lower the quality of your life—or interact with the people who bring negativity around. Here's the bottom line: Your not-to-do list is just as valuable as your to-do list, and it's the secret to being high-performance all the time.

EXERCISE

I want you to create a not-to-do list by asking yourself a simple question: "What am I not delegating to others that I don't need to be doing myself?" It might take you some time to answer the question. Resist the urge to hold onto stuff that's currently on your to-do list. Think of this as spring cleaning for your to-do list.

CHAPTER SEVEN

What Do You Think? I Don't Know, What Do You Think?

THERE WAS A BUSINESS I was involved with for a short period that was run unprofessionally. One small example: I was a district manager at this company, and when it was time for the bimonthly paychecks to go out, I'd be sent a big stack of them to distribute. Almost as soon as I received the stack, I'd get a phone call: "Bedros, um, could you hold off on distributing those paychecks for a bit? We don't have money in the account right now." This was a big enough company that this practice seemed especially shady. But I was young, and I wanted to do well, so I didn't say anything.

I of all people understand how companies can find themselves on the razor's edge, but this went on for six months. Each time there'd be some new set of excuses. The employees would get paid . . . eventually. A lot of times, though, their checks would bounce. Even my own paychecks were bouncing. I think I felt loyal, or maybe I was just too scared, or both, so I didn't say anything to anyone high up in the organization. But because I was the boss of all these people in my district, I also internalized the anxiety of having to give out these checks. Month after month, I'd say to myself, "Should I quit? Should I stay? Should I say something? Should I report them?" I couldn't make a decision, and week after week went by with the stress building up. It came to a head one day when I found out I had a bleeding ulcer in my stomach. The stress had actually caused my gut to rip open. I couldn't digest my food properly anymore. I could only eat one small meal per day. And I was popping antacids like crazy the rest of the day just to quiet my stomach.

I knew I should have quit, but I didn't. I was indecisive, and I'm convinced that those months took years off my life.

That's not the only time I've struggled with indecision. In the early years of Fit Body Boot Camp, I delayed making decisions about the structure of the business that ended up costing me almost half a million dollars. When we first launched FBBC in early 2010, it was a licensing program and not a franchise. I'll save you the details and legalities, but it's important for you to know that there are certain distinctions that the government in the state you're operating out of looks at to determine if you are operating as a franchise or a licensing program. One of those distinctions was the fact that we were assigning "territories" to our licensees. We did this to make sure that two FBBC locations did not open up within three to five miles of each other, thereby competing and creating an adversarial relationship.

Another factor was that we asked our FBBC owners to charge the same price to maintain price integrity and brand quality. Now, we did these things to ensure the success of our brand and the service that we delivered. However, the state government looked at it as though we were operating as a franchise without actually being registered as a franchise. And that was a big no-no. I must admit that I had a feeling that we had crossed the line from licensing to franchising in the spirit of delivering better service, but we weren't 100 percent sure of this fact. Rather than doing the research, figuring it out, and then hiring an attorney to help us officially become a franchise, we decided to take a wait-and-see approach—this is what indecisive people do.

Honestly, I don't know why I was so indecisive, but in those days each time I was at a fork in the road and it was time to make a decision I just paused and never really pulled the trigger. Maybe it was fear of the unknown and the process we'd have to go through to become a franchise. Maybe it was the cost of becoming a franchise that got me to procrastinate. Whatever it was, it backfired in the spring of

2011 when the great state of California sent us a notice informing us that they were considering charging us a $2,500 fine per location and that we were not allowed to sell another location until this issue was resolved. Shit!

At the time, we had just over 180 Fit Body Boot Camp locations. That's $450,000 in fines, which was $450,000 that I did not have—which is exactly what we told the state of California. Thank God the state came back to us saying that they would waive the fines since it was an honest mistake on our part. But there was one condition: We had to agree that we would not sell another location until we were officially franchised. For the next eleven months, we didn't sell a single location while we went through the franchising process. We ended up losing over $150,000 in new business because we were unable to sell locations until we could show the state of California that we were officially franchised in all the states. I suppose that losing $150,000 in new business is a lot better than getting fined $450,000. But the whole thing could have cost me $40,000 had I decided to research, take action, and hire an attorney to convert Fit Body Boot Camp into a franchise. Indecision cost me a lot of money, grief, and headaches that time. It wasn't the first time that indecision cost me—and it wouldn't be the last.

The bottom line: Not making a decision is often worse than making a bad or wrong decision. In fact, not making a decision *is* making a decision. It allows circumstances to make the decision for you. Indecisiveness gives control of your outcome to others. Being indecisive is a business killer and it's a personal killer. Weak leaders procrastinate so much on a decision that by the time they make it they've already lost the opportunity, time, money, respect, or the element of surprise that they needed to crush their competition. They end up broke and stressed and they struggle throughout their entrepreneurial careers. Ironically, the reason they don't make decisions is because they look at decisions as risks and they attempt to get all the facts before making a decision.

I've got news for you: You've chosen to be an entrepreneur, therefore you're in the risk-taking business! You simply can't wait to gather all the facts and information you need before you can make a decision. At best you're going to have a fraction of the information you need at any given time and you better be okay with making a decision in those situations. The faster you can make a decision, the sooner you'll find out if it's the right decision or not. If it's right, then you stay the course. If it's not, then you course correct. One indicator of high performers and effective leaders is that they are incredibly decisive. Notice: I didn't say that strong leaders make the *right* decision every time. I said that they are incredibly *decisive*.

President George W. Bush wasn't wrong when he said that as president he was "the Decider." That's basically the whole job: to make the calls and own the consequences. The best thing you can do as a leader is make fast decisions. Over time you'll begin to develop your gut decision-making skills and you'll end up making better decisions more often. It's a game of repetition. As an entrepreneur, speed of implementation is king. If you and I are competitors in the exact same industry, and we go to a marketing conference where we learn a new and revolutionary lead-generation strategy, then it comes down to this: The business that can pull the trigger and execute the marketing strategy the fastest will dominate the market. Make a decision, make it fast, and kick ass!

I've had other moments in my life when making a quick decision, saying yes, and getting going has proven lucrative. One of the best examples is a business I built that automated the sending out of emails for personal trainers. At the time, I was sending out emails to gym owners about how to run their businesses and what the best marketing tactics were in our industry. Twice a week, I'd hit up their inboxes with tips, suggestions, guidance, and lessons learned. A lot of them would write back saying things like, "Man, I wish I could do this as consistently as you for my personal training clients."

So one day I woke up and said, "Okay, let's build an email delivery platform for the fitness industry that will automatically send out content-rich emails to their clients and prospects once a week." I didn't know anything about software developing. I didn't know what to do exactly to get this thing to market. But I knew that this was going to be a winner if I could get it into the hands of my customers. Now I could have spent time researching programming companies, emailing delivery platforms, and interviewing content writers. And all that research would have led to more fact-finding research, which would have led to my losing motivation and giving up on the idea once I discovered how much it was going to cost. Or I could pull the trigger, get the ball rolling, and figure it out as I went. I did a Google search for "software programmers," found a company out of India that was able to do the job for me at the price I wanted, and off we went. Once I made the decision to do the Google search and hire the programing company a lot of other elements fell into place, because each time we came to a fork in the road I made a fast decision. That business, FitPro Newsletter, still exists today and generates over a million dollars a year for me on autopilot.

If you find something you're excited about but don't take immediate action on, you're probably searching for problems and finding reasons not to do it. The longer you wait, the less likely you are to pull the trigger. You'll lose morale, speed, and enthusiasm. That's why great leaders decide quickly and move on. In his biography, General Colin Powell talks about his 40/70 rule. He says that to make a decision, great leaders need as little as 40 percent of the information and no more than 70 percent. In other words, those who wait to gather 100 percent of the information and facts before making the decision end up losing the edge in business and in life.

So how do you become more decisive? Well, as it turns out, you can become more decisive by building your decision-making muscles. First, I want you to realize that the reason you're indecisive right now is because you're probably assuming that a bad decision is going to result in catastrophe and chaos. The reason you feel that way is because you're operating out of a place of fear, doubt, and uncertainty. Rarely does a single decision lead to total chaos and failure. So you can stop overthinking that fact. Ironically, the way you become a confident and certain leader is by being decisive and using speed of implementation to your benefit.

Look, there's nothing scary about making a bad decision. When we make decisions, they either work out, or they don't. What you imagine is going to happen, as a by-product of making the wrong decision, is often far from reality. And more than that: Indecision is a choice. When you don't make a decision, you end up letting circumstances decide for you. Typically, that's not going to be a favorable outcome.

I give you permission to make a decision. If you figure out that it was the wrong decision, then you can quickly course correct. Stop freaking out over little things. Lebron James may have put this best: "I always say, decisions I make, I live with them. There's always ways you can correct them or ways you can do them better. At the end of the day, I live with them." Make your decisions. Live with them. Because fretting doesn't undo anything and wishing doesn't change the future.

The Six Pillars of Effective Entrepreneurial Leadership

PILLAR #3: DECISIVENESS

Decisiveness is your ability to make decisions quickly and under pressure when you don't have 100 percent of the information required. It's something that all entrepreneurs need, and it starts with the small things in life: What shirt do I wear today, where should we go to eat, what time am I working out, Lyft or Uber, sushi or steak, shorts or pants? Make these small decisions quickly so that when you come to a fork in the road where a big decision needs to be made, you can make it swiftly and confidently.

It's easy to get stuck when you simply don't have all the information that you feel is needed to make a decision, and for entrepreneurs that happens more often than you'd imagine. Always make a decision. Your instincts will tell you to drag your feet and wait until new information is available, but waiting is hardly ever the smart move.

Colin Powell, former head of U.S. military forces and former secretary of state, created the 40/70 rule to help get through the fear that comes when faced with a big decision. Again, his rule states that you only need between 40 to 70 percent of the information to make a decision. Less than 40 percent of the information is insufficient to make a good decision and waiting for more than 70 percent of the information is a waste of time. If it turns out that you made the wrong decision, then you simply and quickly pivot with the new information received.

How Decisiveness Serves You

A company that makes good decisions quickly has a higher metabolism, which allows it to act on opportunities and overcome obstacles.
—Paul Rogers and Marcia Blenko, "Who Has the D?
How Clear Decision Roles Enhance Organizational
Performance," *HBR's 10 Must Reads
On Strategy* (2011)

Decisiveness is a vital skill for you to master since the landscape moves fast, the industry moves fast, and technology moves fast. If you wait to make a decision, or freeze up and refuse to make a decision, a decision will be made for you—and it won't be made in your favor.

This ability transfers into business and your personal life and to the big decisions that come along, and it allows you to pivot around obstacles with quick decisions rather than taking a wait-and-see approach, which leads to loss of speed and market share.

EXERCISE

As I said, I want you to become decisive and build your decision-making muscles. I want you to make fast decisions. You can start by doing this as a fun little game with your friends. If you and your friends are trying to decide what you're going to do on Saturday night, then I want you to act fast, be decisive, and tell the group of friends exactly what you're going to do. You'll be pleasantly surprised to find out how much they appreciate your decisiveness and you'll quickly see how they look up to you as a leader.

Or how about the next time you're on a date trying to figure out where to go for dinner, and you and your date are playing the "where do you think we should go" game. Don't hem and haw. Be decisive, make the call, and get that date going already!

Or the next time you're going to pick an outfit to wear, make the decision fast, stick to it, and do not waver. Getting good at making these little decisions quickly and with confidence will help you make the bigger decisions in life quickly and with confidence. Remember that at the end of the day, the person who makes the fastest decision ends up winning the game.

Make decisiveness a new habit.

CHAPTER EIGHT

Why You Should Never Sleep with the TV On

S ARAH WAS A FASHION CONSULTANT and one of my coaching clients. She was struggling in her business in a very particular way. Like all entrepreneurs, Sarah encountered occasional challenges, setbacks, and unexpected financial burdens. She had been an entrepreneur long enough to have gone through several phases of growth and had already experienced many obstacles. What I noticed about Sarah, though, was that she continued to react to each setback as though this was the absolute end of her business.

Her responses were out of proportion with the challenges. During one of our mastermind meetings, someone brought up the topic of sleep and how as entrepreneurs we sometimes don't get enough sleep to feel rested for the next day's challenges ahead. Sarah quickly chimed in and volunteered the fact that she simply did not sleep well at night and needed to figure out a way to get better sleep. She went on to say that having the TV on in the background seemed to help quiet her mind so she could fall asleep and stay asleep.

That was the golden thread I had been looking for.

I asked Sarah what she watched as she fell asleep.

"Oh, one of the cable news channel shows," she casually responded.

"Do you think having the news channel on all night while you sleep is causing you to experience a disproportionate amount of anxiety and stress in your work?" I asked, though it was one of those instances in which I already knew the answer. I just wanted her to arrive at it herself.

At first, she wasn't able to connect the dots, and I can understand why. The concept of having the TV on all night while you sleep and then being emotionally charged and on edge the next day isn't something that's easy to connect. So I broke it down for her.

"Sarah, your subconscious mind is always recording everything around you. When you fall asleep with the news networks on all night, your subconscious mind is recording all the negativity that they are reporting on from around the world. As an entrepreneur, you've got an obligation to keep your mind safe from negativity that can influence your belief system and ultimately your day-to-day habits and actions."

Have you ever had a dream where you were falling and then woke with a start as though you actually fell off the bed? That's your mind incorporating what's happening around it into your reality. When the talking heads on TV are reporting on the cost of the war, the impending doom of the economy, inflation, murders, and crimes, don't you think that your subconscious mind is recording it all and operating from a place of hopelessness, fear, and uncertainty? Of course it is! That's how subliminal messaging works: Information is fed into your subconscious mind, and that information then controls your belief system and that controls your habits, which control your actions. All the while you believe that you're making conscious decisions, when in reality those decisions have been made for you. So if your subconscious mind is consuming negative and fear-based information, then it's going to amplify your reactions to the normal challenges and setbacks that happen as an entrepreneur.

Feeding your mind negativity by watching the news, listening to it on the radio, reading it on the internet and in newspapers, and gossiping about it with people creates a negative outcome and a fear-based mind-set. And that's not what decisive and effective leaders are made of.

After our discussion, Sarah stopped sleeping with the television on. And lo and behold, after she changed this habit, she realized that her emotional reactivity went down and that her ability to handle setbacks went up. Now she responds with confidence, clarity, and courage to each situation presented to her. Best of all, her employees now respect her and are on board with her vision. Getting rid of the late-night TV wasn't the only change Sarah made: She also made the commitment to be in bed by 10 p.m. each night and not stay up late to watch TV, scroll through social media, or check emails. She wakes up at five and works through her attack list without disruptions. She focuses on self-care by getting in forty-five minutes of exercise five days a week and eating healthy foods that are low in sugar and starches and high in protein and fiber.

As Sarah evolved into a strong, capable, and decisive leader, she began to develop a clear picture of how she wanted her business to look, where she wanted it to go, and how it was going to get there. This wasn't by accident. Your mind is your day-to-day decision-making computer, and just like a computer, if your mind is infected with a virus it will perform poorly. In Sarah's case, the virus was the subconscious messaging of late-night news. But everyone has a version of the virus in their lives that they need to get a handle on.

Another way to look at your mind is from a "tip of the iceberg" perspective. The tip is your conscious mind. That's the mind you use when you decide whether you're going to have sushi or steak for dinner. The conscious mind is also used for simple day-to-day decisions like: Long or short sleeves today? Coffee or tea? Stairs or the elevator? etc. But the thing that controls your big, important decisions is the larger, hidden part of the iceberg. This is your subconscious mind. Your subconscious mind is always recording the environment around you and influencing your belief system. And the things that you believe are the things that you will manifest in life.

Everyone has a soundtrack that plays in their head. This soundtrack plays on a continuous loop and has tremendous influence on your subconscious mind that then determines your belief system and your actions. What soundtrack is playing in your head? For most people, I suspect it's a negative self-talk loop. That they are not capable, not deserving, not worthy of money or success. Or that the competition is too steep, the economy is too volatile, and the market too disjointed. This negative self-talk soundtrack could be installed by your family, upbringing, trauma, negative childhood experiences, friends, or your circle of influence.

You can't expect to have amazing experiences and outcomes if the soundtrack in your mind is negative and self-limiting. So how do you fix this? Read books, listen to audio programs, and reprogram your mind with positive, uplifting messages. There's an entire industry devoted to personal development. Just pick up a book or podcast and dive in. Surround yourself with positive and optimistic people. After all, you are the sum of the five people who you surround yourself with the most. By making these shifts you will change the soundtrack into one of positive self-talk, and that leads to an optimistic belief system, which leads to actions that produce successful outcomes. Like anything else, this isn't a onetime thing. You have to do this over time, through repetition, just like the negative thoughts that were reinforced and installed in your brain through repetition. But if you do the work, you will achieve the outcome.

The Six Pillars of Effective Entrepreneurial Leadership

PILLAR #4: EMOTIONAL RESILIENCE

Being emotionally resilient will make anyone's life easier and happier, and I believe that it's important for the entrepreneur to have an even higher degree of emotional resilience than the general population.

Emotional resilience helps you successfully handle all the responsibilities and unpredictability of your entrepreneurial life. You're trying to stay ahead of the curve. You're keeping an eye on the economy, your employees, your competitors, and your clients and customers. You may have an employee who quits and takes company information to a competitor. You may be fined by the Federal Trade Commission. You may experience an economic downturn in your particular industry that forces you to take out a line of credit on your home.

All these challenges are a trigger for anger, depression, and emotional turmoil. Without emotional resilience, you end up going into a limbic state where panic and stress take over. While limbic, you're not clearheaded enough to make a decision that will benefit the longevity of your business. You may fire off an angry email to a customer or a passive-aggressive text to your employees or business partner.

Emotional resilience makes it possible to move from reacting to situations aggressively with rage, fear, and doubt to, instead, responding effectively.

How Emotional Resilience Serves You

Emotional resilience means having the ability to control your emotions when the suck factor comes. It means taking a step back and a deep breath to ask, "Is this person doing this *to* me, or is it just happening and it's merely a problem that I need to solve?"

Take an hour or two—or a day or two, depending on the severity of the challenge—to think about the problem. You'll come up with three to five really effective solutions versus being stuck in that emotionally limbic state that damages your reputation, your leadership, and the trust that people have in you.

EXERCISES

Here's my three-part way to break out of the pattern of negative self-talk. It's bulletproof; I guarantee you this will work. Give it a shot the next time you find yourself caught in a cul-de-sac of negativity.

1) Change Your State

Massive credit to Tony Robbins on this one. The easiest way to change your thoughts is to change your state. So what do I do? I stand up, put a smile on my face, think about a time when I had a great experience. I do anything I can to change the state I'm in to change the thoughts I have. Sometimes I jump up and down and just say, "I like myself, I like myself, I like myself!" Yeah, it sounds silly, and sometimes I laugh at myself. But it works! The blood flows, the endorphins go, and boom, I'm in a more positive state of mind.

I learned a great example of this from my mentor Jim Franco. As I was getting to know him, he invited me to his office and gave me a tour. I noticed that on each of the cubicle walls for his customer support reps was a mirror at face-level. Underneath was a little sign that said, "Smile." I asked Jim why he did that. And he told me, "It's been proven that if you smile even over the phone, people can feel that energy. They can feel the lightheartedness." It's a lesson I've never forgotten.

2) Get a Little Win

Feeling down about one task and stuck? Pick a task you're good at and get a win. Sometimes in the middle of a tough business issue or problem, I'll just walk into my gym and throw a kettlebell around. Or I'll go to the backyard and start flipping a tractor tire for exercise. Why? Because it's something I'm good at. I'm strong and active and this is something I can get an "easy win" with. The negative part of my brain that's focused on the *other* problem shuts down and the positive part fires up. When that happens, I usually find more and better solutions to my problems.

3) Show Gratitude

Take two minutes and ask yourself, "What am I grateful for right now?" And just list them and go through each one. Take in the list, *feel* it, and show real appreciation. Oftentimes we get so caught up in the details that we forget to show gratitude for the awesome lives that we have. Show and feel real appreciation for each thing on your list and you'll see how quickly you can go from a negative to a positive state of mind.

Your Vision and Path

I F YOU DON'T KNOW where you're going, how will you get there? If you don't know why, how will you get through the bumps, bruises, and setbacks? If you don't know the path, how will you avoid wrong turns?

If you don't have a clear vision for your business, a clear path for how you will get there, and a clear "big reason why" for it all, you're in for one hell of a bumpy (and lonely) ride. I'm going to help you get clarity on all three, starting right now.

CHAPTER NINE

Picking a "Just Right" Purpose

ALFWAY THROUGH MY FRESHMAN YEAR of high school, I got kicked out. I was in a fight. I didn't start it (I swear!), but the school had zero tolerance for fighting, so I was expelled. I had to start over and make new friends at a new high school.

I wasn't Mr. Popularity. Part of that was because I was heavy, like with thirty pounds of extra fat. I had no confidence, which meant I'd keep to myself and had a difficult time making friends. A poor diet and no exercise will do that to you. Growing up we didn't have a lot of money, so we ate whatever we could get our hands on. I ate a ton of processed food, white bread, and assorted snacks—and if a plate had food on it, I just ate it. When you grow up poor, with a scarcity mind-set, and you aren't sure where your next meal will come from, you just eat whenever there's food around, whether you're hungry or not.

So I was overweight. I had man boobs. I had a belly that hung over my belt line. I had love handles. I had chunky cheeks. Well into my sophomore and junior year, people wouldn't talk to me, and I connected it to my looks and my weight. Thankfully, one of the students in my sophomore science class, Darren, was a football player and he ended up as my lab partner. I told him how I hated being out of shape and that I wanted to work out and get in shape. I asked him about eating right and what the best way was to get fit.

I'll be honest: I was asking him because there was a girl I had a massive crush on. I wanted to take her to prom the following year. But looking the way I did, I knew I couldn't. So I wanted to get myself in shape to ask her out to prom. Darren took me to the school gym and put me under a bench press. The bar wobbled when I lifted it, and I could barely do three reps with an empty bar. I felt defeated, and I didn't stick to it. He told me to eat higher protein and lower carbs. I tried that, too, but I gave up easily. I was too lazy to do the work, even though I badly wanted the results.

The summer before my senior year was a wake-up call, a precursor to manning up. Darren had given me the road map, and he had even walked down the road with me for a few steps. But my laziness meant that although senior year was approaching, I was no closer to getting the prom date I wanted. It was ninety days until the start of school—and I decided to go all in. I bought a bunch of *Muscle & Fitness* magazines, and they finally lit a fire under me. I studied those magazines, learned the movements, the intervals, the different lifts and exercises. I worked out for four days and took one day off. This is called a four-day split. I changed my diet, too. I lived on canned tuna and green apples. I kept carbs to just before and just after my workouts and ate only proteins and veggies the rest of the day. Through all that hard work, I lost the thirty extra pounds of fat. I came back to school a new man.

The good news: The feeling of being disciplined stuck. I loved it. I enjoyed the process of working out. I loved keeping a workout log. I liked planning out my meals. It all gave me some hope that I wasn't a fat, lazy, undisciplined foreigner kid who would never make anything of himself. That ninety-day summer of pain and working out changed my trajectory forever.

The bad news: I never did ask that girl to the prom.

▶ ▶ ◀ ◀

In the back of one of those muscle magazines was an ad. It said, "Get certified as a personal trainer. Get paid $100/hour training clients." I did the math in my head and very quickly thought, *This is a gold mine!* Or at least it was compared to my prospects at the time. My life was looking like it was going to be a lot like a friend of our family's: I was going to graduate high school and be a car mechanic. It wasn't a bad gig—I liked cars—but it paid very little. By spending that summer working out and coming across that ad in the back of the magazine, it opened up the door to becoming a fitness coach, all of which led me to the work I do now.

My purpose when I started out seems small: Get fit so I can get the girl. It seems especially small compared to the size and reach of my business and my international fitness franchise. But the truth is, when I was in high school, getting the prom date seemed like a big purpose to me. I was overweight. I had self-esteem issues. I had all kinds of insecurities. So the ideas of "getting a six-pack" and "asking that girl out to prom" were big, inspiring, earth-shaking purposes.

And you know what? They led to action. I did something. I learned how to eat right and get to the gym consistently. I couldn't have used the language of purpose or discipline back then—few high schoolers can—but I knew somewhere in my gut that the workouts connected to the weight loss and the weight loss connected to the prom date.

The path that started with that goal has led me to inspire, coach, and equip millions of people to also lose fat and get into the best shape of their lives. My path then led me to owning and operating a personal training business—something that I did so well that other personal trainers soon came to me for advice and coaching in their own businesses. But I didn't start out knowing that would happen. As Steve Jobs said in his now-famous commencement speech, you're only going to "be able to connect the dots looking backwards." I didn't know then, and couldn't have known then, that my purpose would go from trying to find a date to building a massive fitness business empire.

I went from changing my own body to changing the health and fitness of people in my community. When I first got certified as a personal trainer after high school, I found clients the old-fashioned way: word of mouth. One client would recommend the next, who would recommend the next. I drove from home to home to visit my clients, working with them in person. I charged $11 per hour, but when you factor in the drive time, I made less than minimum wage. That led me to join a big-box gym as a personal trainer—which was what led to meeting my business mentor, Jim Franco.

But my journey wasn't done yet, and I hadn't quite developed the purpose I have now, though I was well on my way. I started out as a personal trainer with the dream of helping my clients lose weight and regain the confidence that they had lost, just like I had done for myself. As I journeyed through this dream, it evolved into a passion for helping other personal trainers grow their businesses by acquiring more clients, thus having a broader impact on a larger number of people worldwide. I was meant for more than what my initial vision entailed.

Your purpose changes with the seasons and chapters of your life. I don't know what I'll be doing in ten years, but I can promise you that I'll be gaining momentum, expanding, changing more lives, and adding more value to the world than I am today. I'm a coach, and I always will be. I started off coaching people on their fitness goals. Then I moved to coaching trainers on their businesses so that they could reach and help more people with their fitness and fat-loss services. As word got out that I was a good business coach and was able to lead my clients to success and profits, more businesses from other industries came to me for help. Today I'm still a coach—only thing is that I coach big businesses and emerging franchises, and I coach the masses from the stage when I keynote at business conferences.

There's a reason I'm sharing all this: You can't know what your ultimate purpose will look like, so in the moment, you should choose a purpose that is powerful enough for you to get you to take action. I think a lot of people get this wrong: Either they set the bar so low that they can clear it easily, or they choose something so impossible that they get discouraged at the first sign of failure. Pick something in the "just right" sweet spot: big enough to get you moving, small enough to be realistic.

Pick a goal that gets you up in the morning but doesn't stop you in your tracks. I'd suggest a goal that is right in front of your nose. Do you need to lose weight? Get on it. Read magazines. Download apps. Hit the gym. Hire a trainer or coach. Get started. Do you need to improve your relationships? Go for it. Read books. Find a counselor or therapist. Start the work. Do you need to widen your skillsets to better perform in your career? Don't waste another day. Read articles. Sign up for an online course. Talk to someone in your field.

Action is the path to passion, not the other way around. In my case, my purpose—get a prom date—led me to action. Little did I know that this one thing would lead me to love and embrace fitness and ultimately develop it into my purpose in life. That's the big lesson here. You're not going to find your purpose in life—you're going to develop it as you go through life.

EXERCISE

Spend some time thinking about a purpose that's just right. Something that isn't impenetrably large but also something that isn't so easy you can knock it out next week. What does a purpose like that look like for you? Why is that your purpose? How will it feel when you're doing it full-time and reaching your potential with it?

CHAPTER TEN

Besides Your Own, Whose Life Are You Going to Change?

I T WAS OCTOBER OF 1993. A few months earlier, I graduated from Savannah High School in Anaheim, California. By this time, I had a gym membership and I went there on a regular basis. One morning I saw a guy on the basketball court who I recognized from high school. Jason was the big man on campus throughout my high school career. His status as star of the basketball team garnered him attention and admiration from the entire student body. I first saw his athletic skills on the court a couple years earlier during a game where he confidently moved around—quick feet and even quicker hands, and always in control of the ball.

At the time, I was an insecure foreign kid with no friends, no prom date, and thirty pounds of fat to lose, so I sat on the bleachers and watched the basketball game with admiration. Now, just a couple years later, I was in better shape and felt confident enough to walk up to Jason and introduce myself to him. The dude was still in great shape. Now more muscular, faster, and still skilled with the ball.

Jason and I started working out together and became workout partners and close friends. He planned to join the military like his father had. He was excited to see the world and to use the opportunity to build a career during his time in service. But when his appointment with the local recruiter was scheduled for 6 a.m. on a

Saturday morning, Jason made a fateful decision that altered his path in life forever: He hit snooze and chose sleeping in over his destiny, missing the meeting with the recruiter.

Just like that the first domino had fallen.

Rather than rescheduling the meeting with the recruiter and getting back on track, Jason decided to work at his day job for another year or so while he figured out what he was going to do with his life. That year turned to five years and before long he found himself five years older and out of a job when the company he worked for shut down.

Luckily Jason had a family member high up in a unionized trucking company who helped him obtain a CDL license and fixed the score of his aptitude test, so Jason got a job making six figures as a Class A truck driver. Yet even though he was making good money, he seemed to always blow through it, buying cars and motorcycles that he couldn't afford and steadily accumulating debt despite his generous salary. After only a year on the job, the demanding schedule of trucking became too difficult for him to maintain and so he quit.

For the next decade Jason went from job to job—from participating in multilevel marketing schemes, to briefly selling used cars, to sitting around unemployed and asking me and other friends for money and job connections. He never held the jobs longer than a few months. By the time we both hit thirty, Jason was still drifting through multiple jobs, fighting off bill collectors, and undoubtedly regretting his decisions from a decade earlier while he numbed himself with fast food and late-night binge watching. My strong and athletic friend who had so much going for him just a decade before had now gained more than one hundred pounds of fat, fell into a depression, and filed bankruptcy.

There is no grand goal for Jason now. He drives a shuttle bus, taking people from the front door of a hotel to the airport and back. Every day is about survival, making ends meet, and thinking about how life screwed him over. In reality, he screwed himself. He once wanted to make an impact by serving his country, but instead he put himself under such debt and stress that he still has to trade time for dollars in an unfulfilling job that will never have room for growth or advancement.

My heart hurts for him still.

IT'S NOT ABOUT YOU

One of the things that's been true in my life for a long time is that my personal vision has almost always been about other people. When I first got started as a personal trainer, I was excited about the chance to help people experience the same transformation I did through diet and exercise. When I grew that business, it was to empower more personal trainers to help more people throughout their communities. Today, my ambition is to get one hundred million people to level up in their health, fitness, finances, business, and servitude.

When I think about where Jason and I ended up, I come back to a simple notion: Jason was always living for himself. Even when he wanted to join the military; sure, it was to serve his country, but it was also about seeing the world for himself and getting a few stamps on his passport. Seeing the world is a nice side benefit, but the military is about service, teamwork, sacrifice, and never leaving a man behind. It's about being a part of something bigger than yourself.

Jason's ambitions were always his own. *He* wanted to look good. *He* wanted to have fun. *He* wanted to own things. I rarely heard him talk about how his actions and decisions were affecting other people, and I think, in hindsight, it was a big part of what held him back from making bigger moves in his career. It's not the only thing—but it's an important quality he lacked.

The most incredible business leaders I know are always doing things for other people, their industry, or humanity. They never think only of themselves. They always think of what they can do for their clients, colleagues, customers, community, or country. The best people on my team are the ones who always walk around saying, "How can I help? What can I do?" (Meanwhile, the worst ones have always thought: "How can I get as much money from this company as I possibly can?") The best people I know—from social circles, masterminds, and in business—are the people who always put others first.

I've tried my best to adopt this mind-set. It isn't easy. I grew up in hardscrabble circumstances, so a big part of me is self-protective. If you come to this country as a foreigner with no money and little understanding of the culture and language, some part of you will always feel like a foreigner with no money. When you grow up wondering about how much food there is to eat, some part of you will always wonder if there will be enough to eat. So I'm not necessarily saying that I'm Mother Teresa over here. I'm only saying that I've worked on my mind-set, and I've tried to become a person who sees the world as an abundant place—and that's served me well.

And obviously I'm not saying I'm *not* a self-interested person: I'm successful, and if I achieve my vision, it'll certainly benefit me and my family. But the reason I get up every day isn't to add a few more zeros to my bank account. It's because I want to invest in my team and give them the best place in the world to go to work and make a real impact on the people we serve. It's because I want to find franchise owners and help them grow their businesses so that they will live a life of financial freedom and abundance. It's because I want to find people in other fields who need mentorship and coaching so that they can reach their fullest potential in income, impact, and influence. It's because I want to be a model of hard work and discipline for my children. It's because one hundred million people are out there waiting for what my team and I can deliver, and I'm not about to let them down.

In other words, my vision might be written by me, but it's not solely about me. This isn't a new idea: I've had the privilege of studying and learning from the best entrepreneurs and self-development thinkers of our time. The one thing that unites each of them is a fierce commitment to the service of others. They want to see others succeed. They know that they themselves will be successful, but where they focus their time and attention is on getting others up the ladder.

You're not just manning up for you. And you can't man up if the focus is all you, all the time. Sure, you're going to have to do a lot of work on yourself, but the way to make sure you have energy during the low points, the way to make sure you have massive impact, is to impact something bigger than you. I guarantee you when you have other people depending on you, you'll approach your work and life in a completely different spirit. Set bigger goals. Be bold in your vision. Aim to impact and serve ten times the people that you originally had planned. If your goals don't scare you, they're probably not big enough.

EXERCISES

1) Make a list of the people, the industry, or communities you want to impact in your life. Next to each one, list the actions you've taken in the last year to help them. Do your ambitions match your actions?

2) Let's say that ten years from now you are receiving the person of the year award by one of the biggest authorities in your industry. Write down in detail what you did, what you accomplished, and why it was meaningful over the ten years that led to you getting their award. Now go out and execute that plan.

CHAPTER ELEVEN

Coming Out of a Crisis

I N 2009, JUST AFTER the big financial meltdown, I came up with an idea for a new business model. I came up with this model out of desperation, but that's how many business ideas begin. Fit Body Boot Camp was born out of a crisis.

As luck (or recklessness) would have it, in September 2007, months before the economic crash, Di and I had purchased a big house on a large property. Truth be told, the only reason we qualified for the loan was because at the time mortgage companies still accepted stated income—that law would change after the economic crash. Had we attempted to purchase that property a year later, there's absolutely no way that we would have qualified for it. So there we were, having just bought a million-dollar home by basically giving our word that we made enough money to afford it and that we'd have the money to pay for the mortgage each month. Then a few months later the economy crashed (hard), and overnight our home value got cut almost in half. Yet another "holy shit!" moment in my entrepreneurial career. And if seeing the house that we couldn't afford in the first place drop more than half its value weren't enough, the day that we moved in, our second child, Chloe, was born.

Now you can probably imagine the fear and anxiety that I felt. I mean, there I was: the proud owner of a beautiful home on a manicured one-acre property in Southern California, with a stay-at-home wife, a two-year-old son, and a newborn daughter. The entire economy was crashing down around us, and I was losing coaching and consulting clients like Milli Vanilli lost fans. After the financial meltdown there weren't a lot of people hiring personal trainers. Of course, if fewer people hire personal trainers, then a lot of personal trainers start to go out of business. And when they go out of business, they don't pay me for my business-coaching and consulting services anymore.

The problem was that, like everyone else during 2007 and 2008, I wasn't expecting a massive economic crash. My expenses were higher than ever—I had just taken on a big mortgage, welcomed a new baby into our family, and signed a lease for a small office space to run my business out of. I had no clue how I was going to recover from this shitstorm. By this point, however, I had experienced several entrepreneurial ups and downs, so I was better prepared to handle this battle ahead of me. I'm now convinced that we can build entrepreneurial resiliency just like we can build muscles.

So, as the economy crashed, I knew I could either react by panicking, allowing my emotions to get the best of me, and letting the whole thing consume my thoughts, which would only lead to inaction and fear-based decisions. Or I could respond to the situation with clarity and confidence. After all, I wasn't the only one going through this economic crash. Surely there had to be other entrepreneurs who had risked it all and had their families on the line like I did. I remember thinking to myself, *I'm not alone and I can get through this, but I have to make some hard decisions and act on them quickly.*

Decisiveness and speed of implementation were going to be more valuable for the survival of my business, my home, and my sanity. That's when I got the idea for starting a fitness boot camp franchise. At the time, most of the personal training industry was mainly offering one-on-one personal training. If you've never hired a personal trainer before, you can expect to pay $500 a month to train with them a couple times per week, up to $1,500 a month for four to five days per week. As you might imagine, one-on-one personal training was cost prohibitive for most people after the 2008 economic crash. The boot camp model made sense because it made working with a personal trainer much more affordable and convenient.

There was strength—and fun—in numbers. Instead of one personal trainer and one client taking up a whole hour, the boot camp model that I thought up would be one coach and fifteen to thirty clients working out together in that same hour. It would make losing weight, getting fit, and having the support and accountability of a personal trainer accessible for most people.

I knew I was onto something big and that this was going to change the fitness industry and the way people exercised. The model for Fit Body Boot Camp made sense, and the thing is, that model made sense for everyone: It allowed personal trainers to increase what they could make. It allowed people who might not be able to afford a personal trainer to work out with one so that they could get better and lasting results. I knew that if I could successfully launch Fit Body Boot Camp as a franchise, I'd not only revolutionize the fitness industry but I would also make working with a personal trainer affordable, convenient, and mainstream. Franchising the business would mean maximizing my impact—to give as many people as I could the opportunity to become fit and to grow a business that they would be proud of.

I was stoked! This was my calling. This became my purpose.

All I had to do was figure out how to turn a business idea into a global franchise when we were in what economic analysts were calling the worst economic crash in American history. I was financially tapped out and leveraged to the max. I had to find a way to sell a few hundred franchise locations to people who wanted to start a fitness business during a recession. I had my work cut out for me.

Once I discovered that it was going to cost nearly $100,000 to make this business model into a sellable franchise, it felt like someone threw me in the ring with Mike Tyson for twelve rounds. But this was my purpose. And I knew it, in spite of all the obstacles and noise in the way.

THE NEXT STEP

It turned out that even though I knew we had a great idea, we simply didn't have the money to hire a franchise attorney or pay the state fees to franchise Fit Body Boot Camp. And so we decided to license it first as a business model until we could afford to turn it into a franchise sometime down the line. My plan was to make Fit Body Boot Camp a platform for personal trainers who once offered one-on-one personal training to purchase a new business model from me and run it inside of a 3,000 square-foot storefront with minimal equipment and overhead cost.

The problem: Nearly everybody was broke. The handful of people who had any money during that time were not about to part with it. Plus, most personal trainers didn't have the money to sign a five-year lease with a landlord for a storefront, pay the deposit, then build out a Fit Body Boot Camp studio inside of it.

Maybe this whole thing wasn't such a good idea after all.

Here's the other thing: Until that point, boot camps were run outdoors, in parks throughout the country, which cost trainers nothing. But I was about to ask personal trainers to invest in my brand, lease a space, build it out, and run an indoor boot camp. I looked at it like this: In the fall and winter months, most outdoor boot camps get screwed by the weather. People don't like to work out in the cold, wet, or snow. So if I could show the fitness industry that my boot camp business-model idea was better because it was weatherproof, systematized in every way, and helped their clients get better and lasting results, I was betting that they'd jump on board.

I knew, having run my own personal training gyms and outdoor boot camps, that if we could solve the space problem and show the fitness industry that this was a legitimate business model, Fit Body Boot Camp would have a chance. We wanted to test the indoor boot camp model ourselves first, just to make sure that we were on the right track before we rolled it out to the industry. That's when I got resourceful: What spaces could we use to prove the concept? Karate gyms? Dance studios? Gymnastics centers? They're all indoors. They're rarely used in the mornings. The difference between gymnastics centers and the other two was important: the floor. Karate gyms often have thin industrial carpeting over concrete, and dance studios have hardwood floors, which are great for dancing but not so much for exercising. Gymnastics centers, on the other hand, have special carpet-bonded foam flooring that's an inch-and-a-half thick, which allows you to bounce around, lie down, and even run on it.

That was the answer. We tested it. We went to a gymnastics center and offered them a small sum of money to use the space in the mornings. We were going month to month. We'd buy our own equipment and leave it in small plastic storage boxes. And we'd find clients from the local area and test the workouts, equipment, and the indoor factor. And it worked! It was a cobbled-together solution, at least at the beginning, but it was enough of a proof point to grow the model.

I started licensing the business model to personal trainers, and I encouraged them to find a local gymnastics center and offer a small payment to rent the facilities in the mornings and run our FBBC workouts. Our first sixty-seven licensed locations all operated out of gymnastics centers that were usually empty between the hours of 5 and 11 a.m.—the peak times that we would run our workout sessions.

This model was a smash success. With very little start-up cost, personal trainers were making money by running our indoor boot camp model inside gymnastics centers, and thousands of dollars in licensing fees started rolling in each month. We were in the black!

I could have waited for the economy to improve before starting Fit Body Boot Camp. I could have waited until we had enough money to come out of the gates as a franchise. I could have waited until we could afford to lease out an actual commercial storefront rather than starting out in gymnastics centers. But if had I waited then, we'd probably still be waiting around for Fit Body Boot Camp to hit the scene. Not having money and having to be creative at a time when everyone around us was losing money and tightening their purse strings turned out to be the advantage we needed to dominate in our space. I've since learned that when everyone else is contracting, you should be expanding—that will always give you the competitive advantage.

IT WON'T COME WRAPPED IN A BOW

The reason I'm sharing the origin story of Fit Body Boot Camp—the story of my purpose and my vision—is to show that they won't always come to you in a tidy way or at the right time. My purpose and vision couldn't have come at a worse time. But opportunity shows up at your door when you're least ready for it. As much as you want things to happen on your time and terms, the truth is that you just don't know when opportunity is going to strike, and you have to be ready to act on it when it does. It's for this reason that decisiveness and speed of implementation can give the prepared leader a distinctive edge.

Another truth for entrepreneurs is this: Your purpose might be connected to solving a problem or pain point for someone else. But that often means you have to experience pain or a problem yourself to solve theirs. It's how you know you're onto something. In my case, I could see it right away: My bank balance was dropping because my consulting clients were losing business, so the first thing to go was me. I had to solve that problem—for obvious reasons—but the solution that came to me was a not-so-obvious one that ended up becoming one hundred times more profitable.

Would I have come to that idea by sitting lotus in a garden with waterfalls around me and birds chirping? No way. There's a great line from former president Andrew Jackson. He said, "I was born for a storm. The calm does not suit me." I've always thought he was talking about me and the entrepreneurs I know! The best of them are the kinds of people who thrive when times are worst.

The broader point is this: You'll get told to "think about your passion." You'll be advised to "meditate on your purpose." You'll get sold on the idea that your vision will just "come to you." That it's about "attracting your purpose." I'm going to go out on a limb and suggest that the number of people who truly have had that happen is far less than the number of people who go around talking about such experiences. In most cases, the successful business owners and empire builders I know came to their big idea because of pain, by taking action and by being obsessively locked on to the idea of making it happen no matter the situation. The most successful entrepreneurs I know simply took imperfect action rather than waiting for the perfect time. They didn't look for their purpose, they worked at something until they developed their purpose. Real entrepreneurs are forged in fire, through experience, pain, and trial and error. Usually there was some crisis that led them to a response, and a business—a vision and purpose—was born.

EXERCISE

One of the best indicators of entrepreneurial success is resiliency. Your ability to stay calm and in control under pressure is critical to surviving and thriving in uncertain times. Think about the last time you had a "shit hits the fan" moment in your business or with your finances. Then step outside of yourself and ask, "If Elon Musk were thinking about how to solve this, what would he do? What would he make? What would he build? How would he come out a winner in this situation?" Write down a few ideas, no matter how outlandish they are, and see how they compare to how you responded.

CHAPTER TWELVE

Vision Isn't a Dish
Served Family Style

B EFORE FIT BODY BOOT CAMP, while I was still running my personal training studio, I came up with an idea for how to lower the cost of personal training so that everyone in gyms across the country could afford it. Technology was the solution. It was a software program that I called Hitech Trainer. It loaded onto Palm Pilots (remember those?) that were handed out to clients at the front desk of the gym. Clients would view their workout in pictures and videos and walk from machine to machine completing their self-guided, virtual workout. It was like having a personal trainer in the palm of your hand. These days there are a thousand apps that do essentially the same thing, with personalization and stat tracking, but at the time (early 2000s), Hitech Trainer was cutting-edge stuff!

I sought out business partners. Jim Franco, my mentor and owner of an automotive software company, was the obvious first choice. He would provide the money and the expertise. Another personal training client of mine was a software designer, and he had a friend who was a programmer; they, too, would become partners in Hitech Trainer. Just like that I had started my second business, but this time I owned even less of it than I had of the personal training company—a measly 35 percent of the pie to call my own.

The Hitech Trainer phase of my entrepreneurial career was filled with incredibly fruitful lessons, though the business itself proved to be a disaster. I soon learned, after spending a fortune in software development, prototypes, and trade show booths, that Palm Pilots can't be safely handled in a gym. They were stolen, broken, and quickly becoming outdated. Taking the software online helped extend the life of Hitech Trainer for another year or so, but the problems with that partnership ran deep.

For one, Jim, my money guy, was shrewd enough to get me to sign loan documents for all the money that he put into the company. Before we were even making a profit, I was paying him back for every penny, plus 8 percent interest! (He was a damn good deal maker and he negotiated a killer deal for himself—and not a great one for me. Had I known better, I could have manned up and challenged him then.) We eventually paid back every single penny to Jim, even though some months we were barely able to make the small mortgage payment on our first house.

For another, I started to feel the sting of resentment: I was busting my hump to make this thing work, and I didn't sense the same level of commitment from the partners. Di and I worked tirelessly creating the extensive exercise database, doing photoshoots, and then building an email list of potential customers. The other partners were caught up in their "real" jobs most of the time, dedicating little effort to make Hitech Trainer grow.

Hitech Trainer was eventually shut down, and the company disbanded. While working on Hitech Trainer, as a way to make ends meet, I started selling marketing and business systems information to personal trainers. It was simply out of necessity because I'd sold my personal training studios in order to focus on Hitech Trainer full-time, and I was quickly running out of money while waiting for the big bucks to start rolling in from Hitech Trainer (and they never did).

So with Hitech Trainer in my rearview mirror, a few entrepreneurial war stories under my belt, and a burning desire to pull myself out of debt, I jumped into my role as the go-to business adviser for personal trainers. The truth was that I knew how to sell and market personal training like no one else, and I had the information that thousands of personal trainers across the world needed.

The internet became my vehicle for providing personal trainers with everything they needed to succeed in their businesses. From information products on how to sell, market, and manage their businesses to an email newsletter software that put their marketing on autopilot, I was the one-stop shop for fitness professionals to become profitable and successful.

As my influence and following in the fitness industry began to take off, my gut told me that being the guy behind a computer screen just wasn't enough. This meant putting on my first live event. Holy shit, the thought of putting together an event in a hotel ballroom, coordinating the details, getting other speakers, creating a schedule, and selling the tickets was completely overwhelming for me and way out of my comfort zone. There was no way that I could do this alone. I was in need of the man on the white horse. Someone to swoop in and do the heavy lifting for me. Enter partnership number three. And, no, the third time wasn't a charm.

That was the Fitness Business Summit. No one remembers that the first FBS in 2007 was co-run with another fitness personality— let's call him Jacob. Jacob took home half of the profits from the event, even though my small team and I did every ounce of the preparation and sales for it. Together, Di, my assistant, my brother-in-law Pete, and I did everything that had initially scared me stiff about putting on a live event: We rented a hotel ballroom, coordinated the details, found other speakers, created a schedule, and sold every single one of the tickets to Fitness Business Summit.

The partnership was obviously lopsided: Jacob benefitted a lot more than I did, and I kept feeling the burning resentment of being in a partnership that was more like a one-sided bargain. It wasn't the last time, either. My business partnership at Fit Body Boot Camp would create the same imbalance.

Once I discovered what it was going to cost to make Fit Body Boot Camp into a franchise model, I had to come up with an alternate plan; otherwise, I was going to become another statistic of the 2008 economic crash. That was when we got into hustle-and-grind mode.

For the next four years I hustled around the clock to sell FBBC locations. I burned the candle at both ends. I was simply in moneymaking mode to save my house and what was left of my business. I offered coaching and consulting services to gym owners. I sold Fit Body Boot Camp gyms to anyone who would buy one. I created courses and information products so that I could have something to sell at a lower price. It was a game of survival, and hell or high water, I was going to survive.

There's nothing wrong with hustle and grind, but I had gotten so used to the chaos, the high speed, and flying by the seat of my pants that I didn't know how to stop so that I could create systems and structure and finally scale my business as the economy improved. Plus, I started to see that Larry, my business partner in Fit Body Boot Camp, and I had different work ethics, and we had two very different goals for FBBC. So rather than deal with the differences with my business partnership, I dove deeper into my work and kicked my hustle and grind into overdrive to avoid the real shit that I needed to address.

Between 2009 and 2013, I worked like a rented mule. I operated out of a place of fight-or-flight, and I was going through employees left and right. They would just up and quit, or not show up to work one day, and I'd never hear from them again. I blamed them, but it was just a chaotic time, and, as I mentioned earlier, I was a chaotic and ineffective leader who was unclear in his vision and communicated poorly. I was indecisive and emotionally reactive.

Through it all, Larry and I somehow managed to make Fit Body Boot Camp an official franchise in January 2012 after nearly getting fined half a million dollars by the state of California for unknowingly operating as a franchise. Becoming a franchise was a ray of sunshine in an otherwise dark time in my entrepreneurial career. There was a glimmer of hope. We were selling franchises here and there, nothing groundbreaking yet, but I saw what the potential could be. I just didn't know how to get there.

I also tried to convert our licensees into franchisees so we could get some traction with the new model. But I had one hell of a hard time doing it. In fact, rather than convert into franchisees, our licensees eventually dropped out from being a Fit Body Boot Camp model altogether and went on to do their own thing. Clearly this was a by-product of overpromising and underdelivering. But I didn't know it then. We had high employee turnover at the FBBC HQ, and that didn't give our FBBC owners confidence in our leadership. Plus, the tension between Larry and me was so thick that you could literally feel it when we were in the same room together. I'm sure our clients felt this and experienced it in our less than stellar service and made the decision to jump ship. Looking back, I would have made the same decision, too.

A lot of other crazy shit happened that led to the dissolving of my business partnership with Larry. On April 10, 2012, I received an onslaught of angry phone calls from Fit Body Boot Camp owners regarding Larry's latest shenanigans. This time his actions had crossed the line, the results of which reached heights that could possibly put us out of business. I was on vacation, in the middle of a family trip to Palm Springs, but I cut it short. That very day we packed up and drove back to Chino Hills to end my business partnership with Larry.

During the entire drive from Palm Springs to Chino Hills, I said these five words to myself over and over again: "It's time to man up!" I drove into Chino Hills with guns blazing and called Larry, telling him to meet me at our office. I started rehearsing what I was going to say when I saw him: *"Larry, this partnership can't go on for another day. This is the straw that broke the camel's back. We have to part ways now."* Those words kept repeating in my head. I dropped Di and the kids off at our house and drove to our office. When I saw Larry there, the words that I had rehearsed in the car came pouring out with a level of intensity and focus I never knew I had—and that was that.

Let me be clear about something: Larry wasn't a bad guy. He didn't have bad intentions toward me or Fit Body Boot Camp. In fact, we were family friends and to this day no one makes me laugh harder than him. But in business he was extremely disorganized, unfocused in his work, and lacked the drive needed to grow a big business. This was the wedge that created resentment in me. Throughout the three years we were business partners in Fit Body Boot Camp, there were

many instances where Larry missed important deadlines, overprom-
ised and underdelivered to our FBBC owners, and stressed out our
employees so much that they lost all respect for us—and their desire
to help grow Fit Body Boot Camp.

Although I was an ineffective leader and lacked communication skills, decisiveness, emotional resilience, and clarity of vision,
I did have a tremendous work ethic and a massive sense of duty
and obligation to our franchise owners. Looking back, it was these
qualities that enabled me to carry the business when everything
else was going to shit. A better leader would have communicated
his frustrations to Larry much sooner. A better leader would have
been clear in his vision for the company and path to success. A better leader would have been more decisive and responsive. A better
leader would have focused on building a stronger team, workplace
culture, and morale. But I developed those skills after the erosion of
our business partnership.

PARTNERSHIPS SHOULD COME WITH A WARNING LABEL

Heed this warning: Most people get into partnerships for the wrong
reasons. Most business partnerships don't work. Listen, marriages
are partnerships, too, and we know that statistically about 50 percent
of them end up in divorce. Business partnerships are, in many ways,
no different than marital partnerships. The problem is that most
people go into a business partnership blindly.

You probably don't think about the personality match between
you and your business partner. And I'm willing to bet the farm that
you dated your spouse much longer before you got married. In business partnerships, it's quite the opposite. You barely know each other.
You think you share the same passion, values, and work ethic. You
assume that the other person will pull their weight and share your
vision. Then you have the kind of rude awakening I did.

I've been fortunate to have a whole series of supportive partners
and colleagues. I've worked with some of the best people in the world,
and today I'm so lucky to have the people and partners that I have in

my life. But for those just starting out, you should know: Sometimes your vision isn't meant to be shared.

This isn't a popular thing to say, but how much of your desire to have partners comes from a fear of not being able to do something yourself? That was the case for me. Early on in my partnerships, I didn't have the entrepreneurial confidence in myself that I have today, so I constantly took on partnerships with the hope that my partner would bring some level of knowledge, wisdom, or experience that I didn't have. Let me be the first person to tell you this: You have everything you need to be successful as an entrepreneur. You must start believing in yourself instead of looking to others to solve your problems so that you can finally man up, get disciplined, and take your business to its fullest potential.

EXERCISE

A lot of people spend time creating the perfect vision for their wife or husband. They don't do this for business partners, associates, or employees. I'm going to ask you to do that: Write out, on one page, what the ideal business partner/associate/employee looks like to you. Tailor it to your circumstances. If you're a solo entrepreneur, figure out what the ideal team member looks like. You need to do this because it'll help you get a real sense for the kind of people you want to work with.

CHAPTER THIRTEEN

Getting to an E-Vision

WAS FULLY IN CHARGE NOW. I was the one calling the shots for Fit Body Boot Camp. I bought Larry out, and now I was stuck with a failing franchise and a small group of employees who had zero loyalty toward me, my business, or my clients. There were plenty of times toward the end of 2012 and most of 2013 that I wondered if taking over a failing franchise was the right thing to do.

Should I have been the one bought out? Should I have walked away from the business entirely? Was this another massive mistake on my part? I went to sleep pondering those questions every night. Or, more accurately, I was so stressed about those questions that I knocked myself out with a massive dose of NyQuil and Vicodin— I'm not proud of this fact.

What kind of an idiot buys out his business partner and takes over a failing franchise that is operating in the red? This was yet *another* "holy shit!" moment for me. I was starting to feel as though I was the king of making bad decisions where business was concerned.

Yet deep inside, I knew why I'd chosen to take over Fit Body Boot Camp rather than letting it die or selling it off. At the time, we still had about ninety or so FBBC locations. True, we were losing FBBC locations faster than I was getting new ones on board, but we still had a fair number of clients who relied on the brand and used the systems that we developed to keep their locations running. I simply couldn't walk away knowing that there was even a single FBBC owner who relied on me. To me, that was like the captain of a sinking ship jumping overboard before any of the women or children could get into the life rafts.

I have my parents to thank for instilling this deep sense of duty and obligation in me. After he got his feet under him in America, my father opened up a small tailor shop in Anaheim, California. This gave me firsthand insight into how my father conducted business. He always did the right thing for his customers, even if it cost him money, time, and energy. He did this to a fault. I can remember times when my mother would chastise him for not charging a customer for a small job like sewing on a button on a pair of pants. He would just tell my mom, "Don't worry. It's the right thing to do."

It was this level of world-class customer service that my father used to resurrect the business that he had purchased from a man who delivered shit for service and gambled away what little money his tiny tailor shop had made. When my father bought the shop in the early eighties, we had only been in the United States for three years. Of course he would've liked to have acquired a business that was more stable. But with what little money he had, all he could afford was this failing little tailor shop, and he hoped he could turn it around.

Over time my father built a strong reputation throughout Anaheim by simply doing the right thing for his customers and by delivering better service than all other tailor shops around town. In fact, his reputation as a tailor was so strong that after just a few years of being in business, when New Kids on the Block came to Southern California to do a concert and needed a tailor, their management sought out my father. He still has an autographed picture of New Kids on the Block hanging in the dining room at home.

The other reason I chose to buy out Larry and take over a failing franchise was because I knew this was my purpose and calling in life. By this point, I was 100 percent confident that my purpose was to help tens of millions of people get fit, lose fat, and live healthier and happier lives by eating right and making exercise a consistent part of their lives. Fit Body Boot Camp was going to be the vehicle that helped me reach tens of millions of people each day. Now all I had to do was figure out how to sell and open up a couple thousand Fit Body Boot Camp franchise locations worldwide and I'd be set!

Purpose and a sense of calling can be amazing motivators. I knew I wasn't going to give up, and I knew this was my calling, but I still had no idea how I was going to grow a fitness franchise and turn it into a global brand. So the hustle and grind continued at a relentless pace. I hustled to sell more franchises. I hustled to make connections with people who could connect me with potential franchise buyers. I maxed out my credit cards and ran a full-page ad in a big national franchise opportunity magazine so that I could sell more franchise territories.

Every day was do or die. There was no financial safety net anywhere in sight. I tried email marketing, social media marketing, and sending postcards to personal trainers who had their own brand of gyms, asking them to consider changing over to an FBBC franchise. Nothing seemed to work. I even called existing FBBC location owners and tried to sell them additional franchise locations. I figured they'd be most likely to buy more locations from us. That didn't work, either.

What was worse was that each time I asked my employees to do something to help us service our current owners or get new owners on board, it was like pulling teeth. They did everything with hesitation, reluctance, and resentment. It was like they were just going through the motions. Have you ever experienced that with your employees? I realized that this was their way of having a silent protest against me. This was their way of telling me to go fuck off. Looking back, I don't blame them—it was my fault and I deserved it.

It was fall 2012, and my stress kept mounting. I felt like a pressure cooker, ready to explode any minute. I couldn't catch a break no matter what. More than half a year had gone by since I dissolved the relationship with Larry and Fit Body Boot Camp was still tanking.

You've probably had the same feeling that I was experiencing in that moment. Nobody left to blame. You're all alone, suffering in silence—and you're not about to ask for help. It was right about that time that Di informed me that this was the least amount of money we'd made in the past three years. I didn't know how insignificant I could feel as a man until I heard those words come from my wife's mouth and saw the worry in her eyes.

It was right after this that the anxiety attack hit. And right after that, I finally decided to stop making excuses and feeling like a victim, to take control of the situation and man the fuck up. I had so much potential in me, and it was about time that I reached it. It's funny how a traumatic incident often gives us clarity and helps us realign our priorities. It was then that I realized that my employees work *for* me: *I'm* the boss. *I'm* the decision-maker. I had allowed them to treat my business like a hobby. It was about time that I put my foot down and set new expectations.

A couple weeks after my anxiety attack, I saw Craig Ballantyne and we got to talking about business and the like. Somehow the conversation turned to the future, and he asked me where Fit Body Boot Camp was going. I was baffled. I had no idea and I told him so. I said, "Dude, I'm just trying to keep the wheels on the bus right now. I don't have the time to think about a long-term vision." He scrunched up his face and looked at me with disapproval.

His look told me everything I needed to know. That weekend, I realized I had had enough. Things couldn't go on like this anymore. So I sat down for a couple of hours and decided how I wanted my business and my life to look and operate. I took several things into consideration when crafting my vision for my business.

On Monday, I sent an email to my employees outlining my vision for the business. I wrote:

> *Ladies and gentlemen I don't think I've ever shared my entrepreneurial vision with you. Our goal is to have 2,500 Fit Body Boot Camp franchise locations worldwide by end of 2022. While we'll have 2,500 locations, we will only have 800 to 1,000 location owners. My reasoning behind this is the fewer owners we have, the better service we will be able to deliver to each owner, and the happier and more successful each owner is, the longer they stay with our brand, the more they will become evangelical about it—and that's how we're going to reach more and more people.*

In addition, we're going to have 1,000 clients throughout my various consulting and mastermind programs. Whether it's through Fit Body Boot Camp franchises or my masterminds and private coaching programs, we're going to help a lot of fitness business owners reach more clients throughout their communities. And that's my purpose on this planet: to help tens of millions of people live healthier and become happier by making fitness a regular part of their lives. For this to happen, we've got to 10× our marketing, build a highly motivated sales team, and quadruple the number of new franchises and coaching clients that we onboard each month. I'm counting on you to help me achieve this goal so that we can help more people and make more money together.

I was excited about it. I was hopeful that someone would respond to it when I sent it out. But I didn't hear anything back from my employees. I was bummed—but not surprised. As far as they knew, this was just another sporadic and emotional plea from yours truly. This time, though, things were different. This time I was clear on my vision, and I knew exactly why I wanted to achieve these goals.

One email response did come back, from our newest employee at the time, Joan. She was hired as my assistant, and in her email she said, "Well, if we're going to get to 2,500 locations, then I better start documenting what everyone on the team is doing so that we can create better systems." I couldn't have known it then, but it would be a game-changing move. Because she believed in the vision, she started to figure out ways to make the business work better. She developed what we now call "alien abduction manuals" for each position: If a team member was abducted by aliens, this manual would help us get back on track. It would list simple things: What does each role do? What are the expectations? How do we measure success? It was all seemingly basic stuff, but I hadn't organized the business at all so it was a big deal. The biggest deal was this: Joan was taking initiative. My vision email had inspired her to take action. And that was inspiring not only for her but for me!

Even though I had yet to become an effective leader, I at least had a clear vision for my business. It started to turn around from there.

And I tie it all back to sending that email. Why? Because it forced me to get clear on what I wanted and where I wanted my business to go. And that meant I knew how to lead the team. Could I have predicted that this would have come by way of email? No. But it came—and it has been the defining document for my business and life ever since.

Having a clear vision does something magical for an entrepreneur. It's what gets you out of bed in the morning when you're going through a shitty phase. It's what gives you milestones to celebrate as you get closer to making your vision a reality. And it's what keeps you going with a sense of relentless obsession even when the suck factor kicks in—and the suck factor always finds its way into an entrepreneur's life.

Think about it. When you first started off in business, you probably had a vision of what you wanted to do, right? Maybe it was a general vision, maybe it didn't have specific details, but your vision for your business was clear enough that it got you to quit your job or to take the leap into becoming an entrepreneur. If you're anything like me, you probably visualized in your head the impact your business would make and the feedback that you would get from your happy clients and customers. Maybe you even imagined seeing yourself on TV, getting interviewed on MSN or CNN, or in a business publication like *Entrepreneur* or *Inc.* magazine.

But at some point you went outside of your vision, the destination got fuzzy, and the chaos took over. I know what you're thinking: *I don't have time to sit down and write out a stupid vision plan.* I can tell you this with 100 percent certainty: Just spending an hour or so to clearly write out your vision for your business now will save you years of stress and frustration and hundreds of thousands of dollars in wasted money. You can't afford not to make the time to write out a vision plan.

When was the last time you wrote out exactly how you want your life to be? How much money you want to make each year? How many employees you want to have? How many vacations you want to go on with your family? Or whether or not you plan to keep your business, sell it, or take on private equity to grow it bigger and faster?

I want you to sit down with your spouse or whomever you value in your life and write a clear vision plan like the one I wrote above. See, when you write a vision plan you get extreme clarity on where you're headed. Even more, when the idea fairy comes to you with distractions, you can think back to your vision for your business, which will give you the discipline to stay on track, rather than to go down a rabbit hole of new ideas.

But no vision is complete without having your *why*. In other words, why do you want to achieve that vision? The secret to a strong vision plan is to have a compelling reason why. You're an entrepreneur, you know how people think, you know how to motivate people; when you give someone a big enough reason why, they will take action. It doesn't matter if it's an employee or customer; when the reason why is big enough and compelling enough, they will take action.

Having a clear vision for your business and a date that you wish to achieve that vision by is absolutely critical to your success. Equally critical, if not even more critical, is the "why" behind the vision. In my vision plan above, I shared my goal to have 2,500 Fit Body Boot Camp locations by the end of year 2022 and one thousand coaching clients throughout my various mastermind programs.

Here are my reasons why:

▸ First and foremost is my purpose, which is to help tens of millions of people worldwide achieve their fitness, fat loss, and health goals through clean eating and consistent workouts. The only way that's going to happen is if I help all my clients and our FBBC franchisees get five hundred to a thousand clients each.

▸ Second, I realized that I didn't want hundreds or thousands of employees (not everyone needs to or wants to run a huge business). Part of manning up is knowing what you want out of life. I'd rather have fewer than a hundred employees who are all hand-selected, hardworking, and in line with my vision. I once read somewhere that the wrong employees in your business are like ticking time bombs. Wiser words have never been said.

- I also wanted to grow my company's annual revenue north of $100 million a year. But I wasn't looking for just $100 million in revenue; what I wanted was a high-profit business so that I could continue to support the causes and charities that my family and I believe in.

- For me, those causes are Shriners Hospitals for Children, The Marine Toys for Tots Foundation, and Compassion International—through which, I'm happy to say, we have adopted more than fifty children (and growing)—as well as programs that help American veterans and their families. I'm proud to report that we have donated to all of these causes since 2007, even during the times when we were financially strapped, stressed to the gills, and wondering how we were going to pay our bills.

- And make no mistake about it, I wanted to make a lot of money so I could provide a great life and wonderful experiences for my wife, my kids, and my parents. I didn't want to ever worry about money again. And while money can't buy happiness, it sure does solve the problem of not having money—and that's a good problem to solve. I wanted to give my kids experiences that I never had growing up as a broke foreigner in this country. I wanted to travel with my family and explore this world of ours. I wanted my kids to experience other countries and cultures. I wanted the best education for them, and I wanted them to grow up confident, with fighter jet instincts already installed in them.

EXERCISE

What's your why? Write out your vision and be specific about the details. Read your vision statement often and let it serve as your North Star to guide you.

CHAPTER FOURTEEN

Clarity of Path

I F VISION IS THE DESTINATION, then path is the vehicle that will get you there. Now that you've got clarity of your vision and you've identified your reason why, it's time to move on and get clarity on your path.

Clarity of path is just as important as clarity of vision. Michael, a friend of mine who wrote a self-development book that became a national bestseller, came to me with an interesting challenge. He was a national bestselling author, and as a result of all his sales, he was given lots of speaking opportunities, and from time to time, he'd get a consulting client from those speaking engagements. Now, you would think that his consulting business would be thriving, but like many bestselling authors, he was struggling to get consistent growth and traction in his business. In fact, Michael had been trying to build his consulting gig for some time so that he could cut back on his travels and speaking engagements, but he couldn't figure out a successful way.

I asked him if he knew what he wanted his business to look like twelve months from now, and to my surprise, he was pretty darn clear on his vision. He said he only wanted to work with people and businesses that were committed to a cause and making an impact, and he wanted to have plenty of time to continue writing. But he also wanted a business that generated between one-and-a-half and two million dollars a year. He figured at that level he could have all the money he wanted and still have the freedom to write his future books, travel for leisure, and pick and choose the clients whom he wanted to work with the most.

When I asked Michael how he was going to get there, he gave me a blank stare and said, "I don't know; that's why I'm coming to you about it." His hope had been that his bestselling book would serve as a marketing piece and that it would get him more consulting clients.

Sadly, the reality about self-development books is that many of the people who purchase them don't go past the first chapter. Few of Michael's readers ever get far enough to be sold on Michael, his systems, or the idea of working with him. What's worse is that Michael couldn't market to the tens of thousands of people who purchased his book because he couldn't get access to their names and contact information. After all, his readers didn't purchase his book directly from him, but from Amazon, Barnes & Noble, and other retailers, which don't provide him with a customer list.

What he did have going for him was the fact that he had a strong fan following on his social media platforms, including Facebook and Instagram. He also had a few thousand people on his email list who had subscribed simply by finding his website. I was pretty sure that we could use his Facebook fan page, Instagram followers, and his email list to drum up a half-a-million dollars' worth of coaching and consulting business. Based on his clear vision for his business, I figured it would be most beneficial to help him launch a mastermind group of his own rather than to offer individual coaching and consulting, which would be a lot more time-consuming for him.

I asked Michael if he would be interested in starting a mastermind coaching group, and he said, "Absolutely!" He liked the idea of working with a group of clients three times a year. This would be both effective for his clients and efficient for the lifestyle and business design that he wanted. So we set out to build a clear path to generating an additional $600,000 of new business over the next twelve months.

CREATING YOUR CLEAR PATH

Here's how Michael's plan went: For thirty days Michael put out a weekly video on social media that delivered content and great value to his fans and followers. Twice a week he sent out an email to his list. The first email of the week included a link to his fan page where people could watch the most recent video that he posted. A couple days later, he sent the second email of the week. This second email had thought-provoking written content that his list devoured. In that second email of the week, he hinted that he was starting an exclusive mastermind coaching program for people who wanted to work with him, in person, on a higher level to achieve their life goals. In that email, he asked the people who were interested in working with him to reply to his email to let him know so he could put them on an interest list.

Over the next thirty days, Michael put out educational videos on social media and consistently delivered content-rich, value-added emails to his list. For the second email of the week, he teased the idea of his mastermind and continued to build an interest list. By the third and fourth week, he had created quite the buzz about his mastermind program, which is exactly what I wanted to happen.

In that same amount of time, we had a new sales page made up with sales copy about his new mastermind, the dates for the upcoming mastermind meetings, and an application at the bottom of the page for those who were interested in joining the program.

I also worked with him on phone-closing skills during those thirty days so he could easily convert qualified leads into mastermind clients. The plan was to launch the mastermind at the end of the thirty days, move all the interested people to the new webpage, and have them fill out an application so they could end up on the phone with either Michael or his manager or assistant. Michael used these phone conversations to determine who was qualified for the mastermind. If a person was qualified, then Michael would go through the process to close the prospect at $2,500 a month for twelve months. All we needed was twenty clients paying him $2,500 a month for twelve months to add another $600,000 to his annual income.

It was a simple plan. For many it may seem too simple, but simple works best. I explained to Michael that this was as clear as a path as he could have toward his vision. Over time, as he got comfortable running his mastermind, he could launch a second group by rinsing and repeating the process that I taught him. There's a big lesson here: Simple works. Far too often business owners complicate the process and path to success, sales, and scale. Overcomplication leads to overwhelm, and that's when shit will usually fall apart.

This process of overcomplication happens for two reasons. First, I think most people would rather avoid the real work by overplanning and overcomplicating the path and process to success. Second, I've noticed that most entrepreneurs believe that the path to success should be difficult and complex or it just won't work. This is far from the truth.

Clarity of vision and clarity of path are all you need. I know it sounds simple, but this is what's been missing in your business, which is why you've been stuck and spinning your wheels for so long. Be clear on your path. Write out the questions below and answer them in detail. Once you have your answers, then you can create the path that will get you to your destination. These might, in some cases, seem like basic questions—but again basic works. Go through them and write down specific answers. If I had to guess, I would say this exercise is going to be harder than you think, but that's the point.

The Six Pillars of Effective Entrepreneurial Leadership

PILLAR #5: CLARITY OF VISION AND PATH

The beautiful thing about being an entrepreneur is that we are blessed with creativity and the ability to come up with solutions to many different problems. But the reality is that you'd need at least eight lifetimes to put all your business ideas into action! You're better off finding the one business idea that you are madly in love with and focusing all your efforts on it. Without clarity of vision and path, you're going to become distracted by your many different ideas and never bring a single one to its fullest potential.

Clarity of vision means asking yourself where you want to take your business, when you want to get it there, and clearing the path to get it there.

For example, with my franchise Fit Body Boot Camp, I am very clear on my vision and path. My vision is to take us to 2,500 locations by the year 2022. The path to getting there is to have current FBBC owners open multiple locations, and for us at headquarters to use targeted online marketing to find more of the right prospective franchisee leads.

How Clarity of Vision and Path Serves You

If you have clarity of vision and path, you'll get your business where you want it to be much more effectively than if you approach it haphazardly. Clarity of vision is knowing the outcome that you want and putting a deadline in place; clarity of path is staying focused on what you need to get there. This focused effort reduces distractions, gives clarity to your team, and eliminates the bottlenecks and distractions that threaten to slow down growth.

EXERCISE

Ask yourself the following questions and answer them in great detail:

- How much money do you need to make each month to live your ideal lifestyle?
- How much money do you want your business to make?
- What are the profit margins you want to generate?
- How does this fit into your desire for meaning, significance, or impact?
- How many employees will you have when you reach your vision?

- ► Do you want a business that gives you a lifestyle or one that keeps you ultrabusy and on the go?
- ► What are the two or three critical things that need to happen for you to get enough clients or customers?
- ► What are the nonessential tasks that you're doing that can be delegated to an employee?
- ► Who's going to make the sales?
- ► To whom, and how, is a product or service going to be delivered?
- ► What are your daily, weekly, and monthly traffic and sales goals?

For most entrepreneurs, big or small, these questions have never been considered or defined. If you don't address these issues, you'll neuter your ability to reach your fullest potential. This is your path. Define it and do it!

SECTION THREE

Your Team

L ET ME ILLUSTRATE how important a strong team is. Imagine a car race. Maybe it's the Indy 500 or the Baja 1000. Crossing the finish line is your VISION, the race course is your PATH, your car is your TEAM, the driver is your LEADERSHIP, and the engine comprises your team's WORK ETHIC, MORALE, and CULTURE.

Are you catching what I'm pitching here? You can have a great product, you can be in a profitable industry, and you can be a world-class leader, but without a strong team with great morale and culture your business will never dominate.

It's important to make a distinction between having employees and building a high-performance team. See, up to this point I've referred to my employees as employees. However, today I don't really have employees working for me anymore. I have a team, and that team is driven. They are high-performance. Like with any game or sport, I'm playing to win, and I want my team to be as competitive as I am.

Listen, if you plan on building an empire and taking your business to its fullest potential, it's going to take more than just you. It's going to take a team, and it's going to take a team who's on board with your vision, trusts and respects you as the leader, and is committed to exceeding your expectations and not just meeting them. Here's how you'll get there.

CHAPTER FIFTEEN

Psssst, You Might Have Crabs!

YEARS AGO DI AND I were invited on an Alaskan cruise by her grandparents. This was in 2004 when I was just trying to figure out how to use the internet to grow my coaching and consulting business. We were financially strapped, and had Di's grandparents not paid for the trip, we simply could not have afforded it. As with most cruises, the ship stopped at several ports. One of these ports was Ketchikan, a beautiful fishing town that sees tens of thousands of tourists from all over the world during their peak season.

As Di and I walked along the water, watching crab fishermen cast their nets from the rocks, I noticed that one fisherman had a five-gallon bucket next to him. The bucket was almost half full of water and inside the bucket were six or seven crabs, each about the size of your palm.

I noticed that one of the crabs in the bucket was ambitiously climbing on top of all the others. I didn't think much of it until this little crab made his way to the top of the heap and started to reach up for the rim of the bucket.

Holy shit, this little sucker was trying to make a break for it!

The crab fisherman was oblivious to what was going on with his bucket of crabs behind him. He was so focused on catching more crabs each time he cast his net into the water that he didn't realize that he was about to lose one of his crabs. I figured I'd be a Good Samaritan and let him know that one of his crabs was about to make a break for it. I said, "Sir, looks like you have a pretty ambitious crab here who has climbed on top of the other crabs and is trying to pull himself out of your bucket. I wonder if you should put a lid on this bucket to contain your crabs."

Without even looking back at me, our fisherman friend said, "No need for a lid. Watch what happens next."

I couldn't believe what I saw. As the ambitious crab tried to hoist himself out of the bucket to win its freedom, all the other crabs reached up, grabbed it by the back legs, and pulled it down to the bottom of the bucket. The scene resonated with me at a very deep and personal level.

Holy shit! I thought. "I have crabs! I have crabs in my life!" I elbowed Di as I pointed down to the bucket of crabs and yelled repeatedly, "Holy shit, I have crabs in my life! I have crabs in my life, and they're trying to pull me down!" (A word to the wise: Be very careful in your word choice with your wife: "I've got crabs!" has a couple meanings. One might lead to divorce.) People may have heard the expression "crabs in a barrel," but it's a different thing to see it in person, to actually see one member of a species pull the other down as it starts to do something.

That moment was a watershed one for me. I knew in that moment that I had to distance myself from all the negative people in my life. Anyone in my life who didn't support or believe in my vision had to go. Anyone who was a pessimist or critical of my dreams and ambitions had to go. Anyone who settled for mediocrity or was okay with just being average had to go. Some of them were longtime friends who I had outgrown but didn't realize it until that moment. If I wanted to succeed as an entrepreneur, I had to eliminate all the negativity and mediocrity from my life.

Among the many traits of great leaders, optimism is high on that list. Colin Powell put it famously: "Perpetual optimism is a force multiplier." This was a guy who had seen combat and fought in wars—and even he believed that optimism could be the difference maker. Always choose to be optimistic. Just like your decision-making muscles, you can build your optimism muscles as well. I don't know too many happy and successful entrepreneurs who are pessimists. In fact, I don't know a single one. On the other hand, every negative and bitter business owner that I've met happened to be a pessimist. I don't think this is by chance.

However, you simply can't be an optimist while consuming negativity. This is why it's critical to distance yourself from as many negative influences as possible. Your thoughts aren't just controlled by TV news, the radio, or the information that you read. The people that you choose to surround yourself with impact your thoughts, attitude, and altitude more than you can imagine. The old line goes, "Show me your network, and I'll show you your net worth." There's a reason that this line has become a staple of basically all high-performers I know: It's true!

When I saw all the other crabs pulling down the ambitious one, I saw a reflection of some of the people in my life who pull me down. I remember when I went paintballing with some old friends a few years after that cruise. During our lunch break, we gathered around someone's car and started drinking a ton of Gatorade and inhaling our food before the whistle blew for the next game to start. It was a hot summer day and we only had thirty minutes to get back on to the paintball field. During some small talk, one of my friends started to piss and moan about the fact that it was Sunday and that the next day was the start of another long workweek. Before long, another friend started griping about the fact that Monday was right around the corner—he hated the idea of it and said how cool it would be if he could magically have one more weekend day.

This was the summer of 2014. I had hired Joan about six months earlier and she was proving to be a hardworking fighter jet. For once I felt like I had an ally at my office and I was trying to do everything in my power to keep her. More than that, she had inspired in me the commitment to structure my life and improve my leadership abilities. I had focused on getting my vision for Fit Body Boot Camp clear. I had gotten my nutrition, sleep, and health dialed in again, and I was doing my best to make the business work. I hadn't felt this way since the early 2000s when Di and I started my coaching and consulting business from our spare bedroom. But now that I had Joan in the office, I was focused on manning up as a leader and stepping into my big boy shoes. I had a renewed sense of hope and optimism that I'd be able to turn Fit Body Boot Camp around with the help of Joan.

So while my friends were complaining about the weekend coming to an end, I was chomping at the bit for Monday to begin! I was dying to put my vision plan into action and do work to move my business forward. Right then and there I realized that my friends and I had two completely different belief systems: They wanted to avoid Monday, and I couldn't wait for it to start.

Now, let me make something abundantly clear: I'm not passing judgment on my friends, or their work ethic, or anything else of the sort. They have a right to their belief system, which was based on the choices they had made for their lives. But my belief system was different. I believed that I was meant to do something big. I believed that I was meant to become a massively successful entrepreneur so that I could do things my way, make a big impact in my industry, and create true financial security for me and my family.

I'm not blaming my past failures on them—obviously, I've been up front about my screwups!—but they weren't helping. There were people who I couldn't simply eliminate from my life, because they were family and I would have to see them from time to time or during holidays, but I chose to "edit" my relationship with them. An edited relationship is one where you keep your exposure to a person to a minimum and when you do see them, you keep the topic of conversation superficial. The trick is to never let them in on your dreams and passions because, as painful as it is to say this, they are likely to piss all over your dreams and punch holes in your ideas. The people who are close to you don't necessarily have bad intentions or want to put your fire out—rather, they are transferring their fears and insecurities onto you.

Only share your big dreams, ambitions, and goals with the people in your life who are positive, optimistic, and have similar ambitions. Those are the people who will encourage, motivate, and inspire you to become the best version of yourself. I give you permission to eliminate, or edit, your relationship with anyone who is not aligned with your vision, purpose, or passion. I can also tell you: It will make an enormous difference in your quality of life, your happiness, and, yes, in your business success.

If you hang out with five successful entrepreneurs, you will be the sixth. If you hang out with five friends who are in great shape, you will be the sixth. If you hang out with five complainers, you will be the sixth. Your mind will subtly adapt to the five people you hang around with the most to gain acceptance and respect from them. So choose your circle carefully. Spend most of your time with people who dominate and have that same mentality, and limit the amount of time you are forced to spend with negative influences.

Now you're probably thinking, "Wait, I'm supposed to cut out people I grew up with and have had in my life for thirty-plus years?" In a word: Yes. Don't make a spectacle of it, but phase them out, because environmental exposure to people with negativity and low energy is contagious, and you have a duty and obligation to yourself, your family, your vision, and your community to maintain the best environment if you plan on building an empire and leaving a legacy.

When you hang out with these crabs, they come with built-in limiting beliefs. Each time you share your dreams and passions and the massive actions that you plan to take to improve your life, your finances, and your circumstances, they will project their limiting beliefs on you, and that's going to create doubt within you. Doubt is the seed of fear, and fear is what causes paralysis and self-sabotage on all levels of improvement in life.

The bottom line is this: You become the sum of the people that you hang around with the most. If you plan on being an optimistic, effective, and decisive leader, then you must find a circle of friends and colleagues who are going the same direction in life as you. Get rid of the crabs. As my friend Joe Polish says, "Be willing to eliminate anything in your life that is not excellent."

EXERCISE

Catch some crabs. All right, out with it: Who are they? Who are the crabs in your life? What do they do that gets you down? How will you eliminate or edit the relationship?

CHAPTER SIXTEEN

Building an Outside Team

THERE IS A PROBLEM entrepreneurs face that not a lot of people talk about: loneliness.

But, Bedros, aren't entrepreneurs always out hustling and going to conferences and meeting people and networking? How could they be lonely? That's all true. But here's how it happens anyway: When you're an entrepreneur, you can't connect in the same way with a lot of the people you spend your time with. Take your employees, for example. You write their checks. You control the business that controls, in some way, their livelihood. So you can't be just like any other employee. You're always at a bit of a distance, so even though you might spend dozens of hours a week with your employees, you'll never be one of them. It's important that you're not one of them, but you still crave the human connection they have with one another just the same.

Family helps. My family is a bedrock in my life. My wife, Di, has been there through the peaks and valleys, and my kids are an instant reminder of everything important that isn't building businesses and growing my empire. As my friend and author Ryan Holiday put it in a piece in the *Observer*, "For all the productivity and success advice I've read, shaped, and marketed for dozens of authors in the last decade, I've never really seen someone come out and say: Find yourself a spouse who complements and supports you and makes you better." I couldn't have put it better myself.

129

But even within your family, you'll often feel a bit of distance. Most people don't know how much entrepreneurs internalize their struggles and suffer in silence. Sometimes you keep things to yourself in order to protect your family. You want to keep a stiff upper lip; you want to be strong. I did this with Di when we went through the worst parts of the Fit Body Boot Camp story. There were things about our finances that I just couldn't bring myself to tell her, because I didn't want her to see me as less of a man or a provider.

So you're with people, but you're on your own. You're surrounded by human beings, but you can't be open with all of them in the same way they can be with one another. As an entrepreneur, you're an island. This is why it is vital for you to build an "outside team." Your outside team consists of people who don't necessarily work directly for you, but they are in your network and in your circle of influence. These are the people who support you, believe in your vision, and push you to become the best version of yourself. Your outside team might consist of a mentor, a business-coaching group, friends who want to see you thrive, as well as like-minded peers who are as driven and as entrepreneurial as you.

I cannot emphasize enough how important this outside team is to helping you navigate your decisions and actions as a leader. Your trusted outside team is there to give you "outside eyes" in the form of trusted feedback or just to hear you out when you're going through a rough patch. And I want to walk you through a few principles about it that you might not know or recognize right away.

1) Your outside team is heavily curated. My guess is that, if you're like most people, a lot of your friendships are ones you fell into. Maybe you went to school together. Maybe you were roommates. Maybe you grew up together. In any case, you didn't necessarily seek out many of your friendships; they happened. And that's okay. Part of the virtue of friends is that those relationships are organic, and whatever combination of time and chance brought you together, it worked and clicked.

The outside team is different. It's not accidental. You need to be very deliberate about who these people are. It's worth thinking about the outside team as a board of directors. You wouldn't put anyone on your board who you didn't (1) enjoy as a person, (2) stand to learn from, and (3) think you could help somewhere down the line. Your outside team will consist of a handful of people who are there deliberately.

2) You won't just "go out for drinks" or "catch up." When I get together with the different outside teams I have, it's often over a meal. But we're not just catching up and shooting the shit. Typically, there's a structure and order to our dialogues, or we're meeting to solve one person's particular set of problems. These conversations aren't idle chitchat. They have depth and meaning and analysis. We're there to talk about business and life and the goals we have and how we're going to get there. Now, we definitely have fun. Some of the best times I've had have been with my outside team. But these aren't your usual groups of drinking buddies. Each of you is going to make a commitment to the other to be a big part of helping that person develop and grow and prosper.

You'll probably choose quieter restaurants. You may even do breakfasts instead of drinks or dinners, just so everyone is sharp. You might go for hikes or do physical activity. It won't be swilling a bunch of beers at the local bar, and that's the point.

3) You'll feel like you've found your long-lost family. Each time I hang out with one of my outside teams, I feel different about myself, my vision, and my future. After hanging out with entrepreneurs or mentors, I feel recharged and have this feeling like I can plow through any challenge that gets in my way. I walk away from our conversations and meals overflowing with ideas and energy and firepower.

To be clear, it's not like my entrepreneur friends are any better humans than my friends or family members I grew up with. They just do different work, have different habits, and approach life with gusto. They went after it! And that rubs off. It also rubs off because they're, well, weird like me. Entrepreneurs won't admit it, but we're all a little weird and fucked up (in a good way). It honestly takes someone weird to go out into the world, leave a good-paying job behind, and say, "Wait, I should build that." It's kind of an insane act. And it takes a certain type of insane person to do it. So when we get together, I feel at home. I feel like I'm with my tribe.

4) The ripples from your outside team will be powerful. Because of my outside teams, I've had the opportunity to travel to places I would not have gone, invest in companies I never would have found, expand my business in ways I couldn't have imagined, and read books I might never have come across. I've met entrepreneurs I look up to. People who make me think, *Holy shit, I thought I was owning it. But* that *dude is amazing!* I've found role models and people who have helped me through rough points. I've also done the same for them: I've been there to give someone advice or guidance or a contact who could help take their business to the next level.

One of the things that makes these outside teams different from just groups of friends is impact. Because of these people, I've taken action. I've done things. Part of that is, of course, the fact that people in these groups are action-oriented. But part of it has to do with the fact that the people who get together in groups like this tend to be very careful about spending their time on activities and with people who are going to do things in the world.

I don't mean to make it seem like we're not laughing with one another or getting to know one another on a personal level. Actually, quite the contrary: Some of these people have become my best friends. They know more about me in some ways than my family does. The difference is that these are people for whom doing something is more important than talking about something. They may be small actions—an introduction here, an investment there—but over time, those little ripples build into a wave of action.

In the personal training world, we tell our clients that you can't out-train a bad diet. In other words, if you're going to commit the time, money, and effort to hire a personal trainer, then you have to train hard *and* eat clean so that you can reach your fitness goals faster and in a lasting way. It's the same way in business: If you're going to put the time and work into growing your empire, then you have to have a strong outside team that supports your vision and wants to help you reach your fullest potential.

See, nobody ever told me about the outside team. I just assumed that all of my friends, family members, and acquaintances would be on my team and want to support me through my entrepreneurial journey. I never once thought that they might doubt me or have their own personal fears and insecurities about being an entrepreneur and transfer those fears and insecurities on me. I'm not suggesting that your friends, family members, and acquaintances are there to sabotage you or that they want to see you fail. What I am suggesting, however, is that factors such as where they are in life and what filters they view the world through will determine whether they're going to be supportive and understand why you're working so hard. For some of them, it's possible they simply won't understand why you're doing this and instead they'll show fear, doubt, and become uncomfortable with your drive and desire to succeed.

Most entrepreneurs don't look at their friends, family members, and acquaintances as part of their team. I'm here to tell you that even though these people are not on your payroll, they have plenty of influence over how hard you work, how high you set your goals, the choices and decisions you make, and the habits that you develop. If you plan on being successful and maintaining a high level of success, then you need an outside team who believes in you, supports you, and expects you to become the best version of yourself.

EXERCISE

Do an outside team inventory. List the names of the people who you spend time with who give you better clarity, make you feel understood, and inspire you to think and dream bigger. How much time do you spend with them? What do you do when you're together? How can you find others like them?

CHAPTER SEVENTEEN

Your Inside Team

Y OUR INSIDE TEAM consists of your employees, but in this chapter I'm going to show you how to turn your employees into an effective team of fighter jets. Your inside team consists of the people who work with you and for you. The job of your inside team is to help you take your business from idea to industry domination.

I'm always shocked when I see just how many entrepreneurs treat their business like a dysfunctional family or a part-time hobby.

If you're going to spend eight hours a day, five days a week, with people, then they better be people who are driven, hardworking, believe in your vision, and trust your leadership. I, of course, had to learn this the hard way. I've already mentioned a bit about how my inside team wasn't everything I wanted them to be in the early days of my businesses. Here's how bad it really was:

- ► I had a bookkeeper who was responsible for making sure our monthly bills were paid. All of a sudden, one day, we started to get collections notices. These were not collection notices for big bills, but for small-dollar things like the electric bill, phone bill, and water bill. Something was up. We had to figure out what. In our research, we discovered whole drawers with crumpled-up envelopes in the back. We discovered stacks of unpaid bills from the phone company, the alarm company, and utility company. When you have bad leadership, even something as simple as making sure basic bills are paid on time can go awry.

▸ I needed to fire an employee who was toxic to my business. It was long overdue, but since I hated confrontation and didn't want to hurt her feelings, I continued to put it off for months, which only led to more damage to my business and reputation. One day I finally got fed up with how she mismanaged my business, neglected my clients, and came in with a piss-poor attitude, so I worked up enough nerve to fire her at the end of that day. Unfortunately for me, she beat me to the punch and quit that same day at lunchtime. Unbeknownst to me, on her way out, she trashed two hard drives containing sensitive company information, changed all our email passwords so we couldn't get into company email, and destroyed the physical franchise agreements that contained client payment history, credit card information, and contact info. These were legal documents that I needed to have on file and they were stuffed into trash cans.

When I reached into one of the trash cans to pull out the franchise agreements, I noticed they were soaking wet and literally falling apart in my hands, and they smelled a little funny. Coffee had been poured on them, along with a gallon of carpet cleaning solution. I called the police. After explaining to the cops what had happened and showing them the coffee- and chemical-soaked franchise agreements, they wrote a detailed report. One of the police officers walked up to me and pulled me aside to ask me some questions.

After a series of basic questions that police officers ask to write a detailed report, he asked me this question: "So how long was it happening?"

"How long was what happening?" I asked.

"How long were you having an affair with her? Something like this only happens when there was an affair and then a breakup."

I literally started laughing out loud! In a moment of so much chaos, stress, and anger, it was great to have a bit of levity. I said, "Dude, I wasn't having an affair with her."

The police officer shook his head from side to side and gave me a look that was impossible to misunderstand: *You're an idiot to have kept a toxic employee for so long.*

► In the aftermath of that, we also discovered that almost one-third of our Fit Body Boot Camp location owners had not been charged their monthly royalty fees for nearly an entire year. In fact, some newer FBBC owners hadn't been set up to get charged their monthly royalty fees, either. In total we had lost $640,000 in income that was never charged. My father, who worked all those jobs so we could live in a single room, would have been sorely disappointed to see me waste so much. I've never told him about it—just couldn't bring myself to. This is the cost of poor leadership, no vision, shitty communication skills, and having employees whom I had allowed to get out of control. I was the only person to blame for this.

These are just the highlights (or the lowlights?). I could go back through a full catalog of all the crazy stories I have. But when I reflect on it now, with the benefit of a few years' distance, one of the things I realize is that my employees' dysfunction was just a reflection of my dysfunction as a leader. I was responsible. I wasn't present. I wasn't leading. I wasn't setting an example. Leadership always flows from the top down, and in this case, the spigot was turned off. So it wasn't any surprise that my employees were cutting corners and doing shoddy work—they took their cue from me.

I caused it by ignoring the red flags and avoiding the tough conversations that I should've had with the employees who I paid to do a job. It was my fault for not setting and reinforcing high expectations and standards. The misbehavior of my employees was not the problem. It was the symptom of the problem that I had created in my business. I was an ineffective leader. I brought on employees who were never given expectations to meet or standards to operate by.

And the few times I did set expectations, I never reinforced them. Yet again, poor leadership on my part. They were never given a clear vision for my business, and so they did what most humans would do in that situation: the bare minimum.

Contrast that with the alternative: When a leader inspires, there's no telling where people can go. One story of this comes from our own business. Crystal was one of those employees who, because they are quiet, you miss their contributions. It pains me to say this now, but before I manned up, and when I was doing a poor job of running the business, I assumed Crystal was one of the bad-apple employees. It turned out she wasn't. She just didn't have anyone to look to for leadership. But once Joan came on board, Crystal took her cues from Joan.

I learned later that Joan gave Crystal tasks that I wouldn't trust Crystal with, and they'd get done. Because I was starting to man up and because Joan was starting to bring some discipline and order to the place, Crystal began to feel like she was a part of a team that was going places. So this employee whom I almost overlooked and dismissed became a superstar—someone who, today, is in a director role in our business and is in charge of our operations, compliance, and onboarding team for new Fit Body Boot Camp franchisees. And this is someone who I might have written off, had it not been for Joan's instinct and wisdom. I once told Crystal, "I had no idea you were this capable." To which she replied, "I don't know if I was that capable, but I just kept trying to keep up with Joan, and through environmental exposure, I started being more like Joan."

People problems become business problems; people successes become business successes. The thing is, very few entrepreneurs think about hiring and firing before they get into the game of building a business. Typically, you get into that game because you have an idea, a product, or a service. You don't think too hard about the process of hiring staff, moving them around in your organization, or having to fire them at some point if they're not a good fit. As your business grows, however, you soon realize that hiring, firing, setting expectations, conducting training, and enforcing procedures are all part of your role as a leader. But if you are the type of person who seeks approval, fears confrontation, or hates to feel like you disappointed someone or hurt their feelings, then you're going to have a hard time firing people or giving them feedback when required.

That was the trap I found myself in. And it cost me in time, money, stress, and energy. I want to make sure it doesn't happen to you.

A FEW PRINCIPLES FOR BUILDING A HIGH-PERFORMING TEAM

Next to effective leadership, your team is the most critical part in your business. Even with extreme clarity of vision and a well-defined path, you will never be able to get your business to reach its fullest potential without a strong, loyal, and driven team. Without a capable team, you will be the bottleneck that stands in the way of where you are and where you want to be. That's a very frustrating place to be. I've been there. There's nothing worse than having a clear vision and knowing your path but not having a reliable team to execute the work. When it comes to your inside team, who you pay and work with eight hours a day, five days a week, you should always stay on high alert.

Where your inside team is concerned, remember this: You are not hiring friends, it's not a popularity contest, and you can't engage in my previous damaging behavior of "avoid it and hope it will go away." The problem will never go away until you do something about it. Either fix it or fire it. You're running a business that costs money, has competition, and involves risk and sacrifice. Entrepreneurship is not a game. You've got a serious obligation to your business, your clients and customers, your family, and your employees to deliver a world-class product or service. Your goal is to hire, build, or recruit a team of highly driven workers who have a can-do and never-quit attitude and who want to win more than anything. Here's how I look at it now. An employee is someone who clocks in a little late, clocks out a little early, and does the bare minimum to stay employed.

I'm sure you can think of an employee or two right now based on that definition. However, a team member is someone who is highly driven, motivated, knows who the opponent is, is on a team of like-minded high-performers, and plays to win.

So then, would you prefer to have employees working for you or high-performance team members?

A few things to keep in mind:

1) The Small Things Become the Big Things

In my earlier period of poor leadership, I would let small things slide. A forgotten report or memo. A missed email. A skipped meeting. A necessary employee disciplinary action overlooked. A skipped conversion. All these stack on top of one another until you have a toxic working environment. I was so overwhelmed dealing with everything on my plate that I didn't pay close enough attention to these small moments. I wish I had. A strong leader makes time for the details.

The truth is, like a cough or a runny nose, those small things tend to indicate a broader thing. They can also be the starting point of a team member's slide into poor work habits or dysfunction. Most often, if you catch these things early, you can have a solid one-on-one with the person to see what's up. You'd be stunned at what it could be. In your head, you might think the team member is trying to screw you over. However, it might turn out that someone in the company is making it impossible for this person to do his or her job. Or that he or she has some big personal thing going on at home that's clouding the work.

But you won't know if you don't ask about the small things. I've said it before: It's okay to be a control freak when it comes to your business. Remember, it isn't just about you. The livelihoods and success of the other team members depend, in large part, on your ability to manage everyone effectively. When someone cuts corners, it doesn't just affect you. It affects everyone in the company.

Pay attention to the small things. They lead to the big things.

2) Figure Out What They're Bringing to Work

I don't mean look inside your team members' backpacks or lunch boxes. I mean this: Remember that just like your personal life affects the health of your business, their personal lives affect the kind of performance they bring to their work.

This is important. A big part of leading a company or organization is being a coach. And one of the things high-level coaches recognize is that on-field performance or lack thereof might be reflective of something happening in their players' lives. Maybe they're going through a rough breakup. Maybe their parents are having health issues. Maybe they've got an addiction, or anxiety issues, or depression. It's not up to you to solve all your team members' problems, but it is in the best interest of your business (and your team members) to be compassionate, to communicate, and to give feedback to help them get back on track.

In some cases, like with Byron's story earlier, you can help them. You can talk to them and coax out of them what's going on—and then develop a plan to fix it. Every Monday morning, I send out a group email to my team members. These emails are designed to do three things: (1) help my team members play at a higher level in both their personal and professional life, (2) keep them aligned on our company vision and values, and (3) give them an opportunity to respond to me, to connect with me, or to open up a safe dialogue. In fact, it's because of these Monday morning emails that I've been able to help individual team members work through anxiety, depression, health issues, and financial struggles. The more I can help my team members, the more they'll help me grow my business and the impact that it makes. The important thing is not to go into the situation thinking you can magically cure everything. Instead, I look at myself as the person who can point them in the general direction of the solution they need while helping them feel understood.

3) Interview for Culture, Not Competence

Some of the smartest people who have ever worked for me were goofballs on the job. Some of the people who didn't have the right pedigree or all of the qualifications have turned out to be rock stars who just needed the right environment of encouragement and support to thrive.

Whether you're building a $100 million franchise; opening up your second brick-and-mortar cupcake store; or making your way in the world of technology, apps, and online commerce, culture is the key. This is why you must hire slowly to ensure that you don't bring on losers who are damaging to your business; train meticulously, so that you can ensure competency and quality of service; and communicate openly and honestly, to keep your team aligned to your vision. Don't just hire on skillsets. Sure, skills and ability are critical, but if someone isn't a good personality or culture fit, then simply do not hire them.

At our Fit Body Boot Camp headquarters, we've turned away people who have had amazing skills in web development, software programming, media buying, and video editing for people who had lesser experience but the right personality. At the end of the day, I can train you up on your skills and abilities, but I can't change your personality or temperament. I'm always looking for driven, enthusiastic, and highly focused team members. I want the type-A, competitive people who have great attention to detail. If I can find those people and they have half the skills I'm looking for, I'm willing to invest in them and teach them the rest of the skillsets they need to get the job done. Plus, those are the people who will ultimately move up in your organization and become a part of your leadership team. You're not just trying to fill a role today. You're looking for someone who has the potential to ascend and lead in your organization tomorrow.

I've seen, over and over again, entrepreneurs who claim to want to hire for culture fall victim to the glitzy resume or the big-titled candidate. I get it. It's seductive. I've been there. I've made those mistakes, and I have the scars to show for them. What I'm telling you is that "hiring for culture fit" is about a lot more than impressive resumes and making sure you can hang out with the person.

Here's how we approach hiring these days: Candidates typically go through four to five interviews before they are hired onto the team. At first, prospective hires are interviewed by a senior team member and the department lead from the department that they will be working in. Assuming they have the skillsets and personality, they are then interviewed by the department lead (again) and the head of HR. Assuming they still have the skillsets and personality by this point, they are then interviewed by someone in our leadership team such as a VP or COO. Assuming they're still a good fit, they are then set up for an interview with me. By this point we've learned a lot about the prospective team members: (1) Are they willing to jump through all the hoops, appointments, and interviews? (2) Did they show up to every interview on time? And by on time, I mean early. (3) Are they consistent with their answers, attitude, and the way they present themselves? (4) Did any of the interviewers catch something that may be a red flag that the previous interviewer didn't catch? You'd be surprised how many times we've found inconsistencies in answers, attitude, and punctuality during our multiple interviews.

The final two interviews are conducted to get a better understanding of the applicants' personality, their sense of urgency, enthusiasm, work ethic, and desire for the job. During the final interview with me, I like to keep prospective team members on their toes to see how they cope with a pattern that they're not used to. I may start off with something like this: "Hi, nice to meet you, my name is Bedros, and I'm the founder and CEO. If you've made it this far through the interviews, odds are you have the skillsets that we're looking for and you were able to convince everybody before me that you are a good fit for our high-performance team. Now I should warn you: You might not like working here. We have high expectations of our team members. We're unreasonable with the goals that we set. We're always operating out of a sense of urgency and great attention to detail. That's probably not the kind of place you want to work, right?"

It's a question that catches some people off guard. Based on their answer to that question, I'll either end the interview or, if they say they're excited to work in such an environment, I'll say, "Okay, then let's pretend that we're two people sitting in a bar, having a drink, and getting to know each other." The rest of the fifteen minutes is spent asking them questions about how they deal with highway traffic, their favorite music, books they've read, movies they like, favorite restaurants and menu items, a time they got hurt or injured and how they dealt with it.

With each topic, I'll ask more in-depth questions and dig deeper, and this usually gives me good insight into the candidates. I can tell if they're decisive, comfortable in a new and unpredictable situation, and resilient when dealing with stress. I can hear if they're clear communicators and determine their overall energy.

Since we've adopted this process of qualifying potential team candidates, we've had people not show up to the third or fourth interview—likely because they overthought it and psyched themselves out. During the final interview with me, I've seen people break down and cry, ramble to no end, and even shut down and just sit there with a blank look on their face. I've also seen candidates that didn't seem like they'd stand out on paper come in and totally wow us in these interviews. But we take our time with all these interviews. We add them to the team with the same care and precision that a GM uses before drafting or trading for a player. Before hiring people, I want to discover as much as I can about them so that we don't end up with the wrong team member on board, which will end up costing us time and money and risk lowering morale. Team chemistry is too important to get it wrong.

Today, my headquarters is full of forty-six high-energy team members whom I consider fighter jets. Make no mistake about it: My team members do screw up like everyone else, but they own up to it, fix it, and make it right. They don't give excuses, and they don't pass the blame to someone else. This didn't happen overnight. It's a by-product of constant and clear communications of my expectations, and it developed through leading by example by both me and my leadership team.

Like all humans, my team members have days where they're off or not so focused. But unlike many employees who get into a funk and stay in a funk for an extended period, my team members have bounce-back-ability. They are mentally tough, they communicate openly and clearly, and they are highly aware of our mission and vision, and because of that they are relentlessly focused on the outcome. Morale is at an all-time high, and that's the glue that holds our amazing culture together.

The Six Pillars of Effective Entrepreneurial Leadership

PILLAR #6: HIGH-PERFORMANCE TEAM

When you start out as an entrepreneur, you'll likely be a one-man show. Then you'll grow to one or two employees, and things are pretty manageable at this point. However, if you really want to become an industry leader, then you'll continue to grow up to anywhere between tens and hundreds of employees. At this size, having a high-performance team in place is the difference between frustrating or average growth and exponential growth.

It's in your best interest to build a team of high-performance team members rather than employees. Yes, there is a difference between employees and team members.

Employees are going to clock in a little late and out a little early. Employees are going to do the bare minimum. They're just there to collect a paycheck and they don't see you as an individual but rather as "the company."

While employees operate on autopilot, team members, on the other hand, are highly driven and detail oriented. Team members are type A. They want to clear their inbox, they answer the phone on the second ring, and they are clear in how they communicate. They're just like you! These driven individuals are *intra*preneurs in your organization. They're motivated to come together as a team to beat out your competition. They want to win. They want to please you, and they are willing to go the extra mile, just like you do.

How Having a High-Performance Team Serves You

Which group do you think will help you grow your company to $100 million? The employees or the driven team members? Obviously, you want the team members.

EXERCISE

Do an onboarding inventory. How do you bring people into your organization now?

What's your process for finding and selecting them? If you don't have a process, build one based on what you learned here in this chapter.

CHAPTER EIGHTEEN

The Glue That Holds
It All Together

THE MOST FRAGILE THING you'll ever have at your workplace is morale. It's the engine that fuels the fighter jets you've paid so much to build and train. Morale is what keeps your team members fiercely loyal and focused on production, services, and sales.

Morale starts at the top, with you. You must cultivate it, protect it, always nurture it, and never let anyone or anything erode it. When morale is high, you win, your clients and customers win, and your team wins. The best visual I can give you of a high-morale work environment is in Disney's movie *Snow White*. (Hey, I'm a dad with young kids. Plus, you know, I actually worked at Disneyland, so I know what I am talking about.) There's a scene in which the Seven Dwarfs are working cheerfully as a team in the diamond mine and enthusiastically singing "Heigh-Ho." No need for a narrator to say, "And the dwarves were working happily." You can see it in their faces! They are jamming. And the best part (if you're a savvy entrepreneur) is that the diamonds are being mined. The work is getting done.

We often talk about the "culture" of a company and how important it is to have a strong culture that your customers and your employees love being a part of. High morale is the glue that holds the company culture together. I believe, in fact, that morale is more valuable than culture.

Here's what morale is: the confidence, enthusiasm, and discipline of a group or team at a particular time. When morale is low, it breeds resentment and entitlement and creates an adversarial relationship among team members and leadership. Walk into nearly any DMV office in the country and you'll see exactly what low morale has produced. When morale is high in a workplace, it creates a sense of camaraderie, flow, and high energy that benefits the team and the clients that it serves.

Morale starts at the top, but it's the team who maintains it, protects it, nurtures it, and passes it along to new team members. Just like love is something that a couple must grow deeper in if they want their relationship to be happy and lasting, in teams like ours, morale must be maintained, protected, and nurtured so that we can preserve the culture that we've created together.

I don't want this to get too abstract, though, so here are ten ways that we build and protect morale at the FBBC HQ.

1) Monday Morning Team Emails

As I mentioned in the previous chapter, I begin each new week by sitting down and writing an email to my team. These emails are written with the intention to cultivate motivation, loyalty, excitement, and purpose in each and every one of my team members. My goal with each Monday morning email is to help my team members develop personally and professionally. Some of the emails are focused on self-improvement, with a core lesson that I want to impart to them. Others are focused on our global vision and the big reason why we do the work that we do. Sometimes I ask for a response from every team member, to keep them engaged and involved in the conversation. This weekly email has done wonders for the tone of my relationship with my team members. I am reminded of my gratitude for them as I write to them, and they are reminded of their importance and value to our organization as they read it. Here is a recent Monday morning team email:

Monday Morning HQ Email (Leadership and Lunch)

Every morning I go through a short gratitude exercise. It's part of my "starting ritual" that I use before I sit down with my Mac-Book for three hours of GSD magic time (new team members, ask your team what GSD means if you don't know).

Here's how my gratitude exercise goes . . .

1) What are three things I'm thankful for in my life today?
2) Who are three people I'm thankful for in my life today?
3) Who are three people I will text or email this morning with a message of gratitude?

This whole thing takes me five to seven minutes to do, but it helps me remember that there is a LOT in my life to be thankful for, even on days when things aren't necessarily going my way. This morning, as part of my gratitude exercise, I had you, my team, high on top of my gratitude list.

Thank you for being so hardworking, reliable, and outcome driven! You mean a lot to me.

ON TO TODAY'S MESSAGE . . .

I get asked a lot about leadership. What makes a great leader and how to become an effective leader? It always turns people off when I tell them that leadership is a process, that it takes years to evolve into a great leader, and that it starts with changing your daily habits from the easy options to the hard ones.

For example, the easy option is to hit the snooze button instead of springing out of bed. Or to cut corners everywhere possible. Or to avoid the talk that you know you should have with someone. Or to blame others and circumstances each time you're faced with a challenge.

But leaders choose the hard options over the easy ones and that makes all the difference in the world.

Leaders go to bed on time and wake up without hitting the snooze button. Leaders show up prepared. Leaders take ownership and responsibility for everything. Leaders are steady in their attitude and actions.

I don't know if you realize this or not, but you are in a leadership position. Whether you're leading the HQ or a department, or a project or yourself—you are in a leadership role.

So how do you fine-tune your leadership skills?

The depth of your leadership determines the depth of your success. One of the best places to start building your leadership skills is with YOU.

Most people would rather know how to lead others into doing their job or how to delegate tasks to those around them. But if you're serious about becoming a strong leader, then you ought to start by leading yourself first.

As I've been writing in my book these few weeks, I realized my evolution into leadership began when I took control of my attitude, feelings, and emotions.

Taking control of your attitude and your emotions is the first place to start. For me, I made the decision to show up with a great attitude, no matter what. Even if I had to fake it, I showed up with a positive attitude and soon it stuck.

Next were my feelings and my emotions . . .

Rather than emotionally reacting or overreacting to a problem or situation, I made the choice to keep cool and to respond with confidence. This has been a game changer for me in both my personal and professional life.

Interestingly, the more I show up with a great attitude and in control of my emotions, the more others want to be around me, do business with me, and help me reach my goals.

Funny how leadership starts with leading yourself into a better place before you can lead others.

See you soon!

B

P.S. If you don't have plans for lunch today, I'd love to invite you to lunch today after your two hours of deep work. It's a bit of a surprise, so if you'd like to join me for lunch, then meet me outside, in front of the HQ at noon today. :-)

2) The Occasional Surprise!

The postscript in the email above leads us to my next technique for promoting team morale, and that is the occasional fun surprise. On the day I sent that email, I had a food truck pull up to our HQ at noon with an amazing lunch for all our team members. It was exciting, fun, and gave everyone a chance to connect. Standing in line outside together, team members got out of their typical lunch routine, laughed with their co-workers, and took pictures in front of the truck for their social media pages. Talk about a memorable Monday!

I make it a point to drop an unexpected surprise on the team every few months. It's always a surprise and always different than the last one.

3) Tuesday Team Meetings: Who Am I and Shout-outs

Joan leads a team meeting every other week in the Learning Center of our HQ. The meetings are opened with the "Who Am I" game. Three interesting statements are read aloud about a team member. (Last time we played, the three facts were, "My parents met when they were in the second grade. I split my head open when I was little. I've high-fived Michelle Obama.") The rest of us get to guess who the team member is. Then the team member in question stands up and elaborates a bit on the facts (her parents grew up on the same street; she fell off her bike; Michelle Obama was on *The Ellen DeGeneres Show* when she was in the studio audience), and we laugh and learn about someone with whom we spend eight hours a day. That brings us all closer together. And when you're close to someone, you're not going to let them down by doing mediocre work.

Tuesday meetings end with the floor being opened for shout-outs. If someone on the team excelled in a way that you noticed, you stand up and give them a public shout-out. At least half a dozen shout-outs are given at each meeting, with everyone joining in with thunderous applause for the excelling team member. It feels great to be acknowledged by our peers. Those team members walk back to their desks feeling ten feet tall and totally motivated to continue kicking ass.

4) Culture Meetings

Everyone on our team goes through a culture meeting. Just as we put our new Fit Body Boot Camp franchise owners through our four-day FBBC University to give them a deep understanding of the business and the systems and teach them how to successfully own and operate an FBBC location, we put new team members through a one-day culture meeting at HQ to teach them the culture of our work environment.

There are four things we stress and teach in the culture meeting:

1) The difference between crop dusters and fighter jets, and that we work like fighter jets—with urgency, speed of implementation, and resourcefulness.

2) How to service our franchise owners and clients. We pick up the phone by the second ring, respond to emails and voicemails within hours and not days, and follow up to make sure the client was satisfied with the outcome.

3) Morale is the glue that holds our fun, competitive, and high-energy culture together. Everyone's attitude, mood, and energy affects team morale, so we all have the responsibility to keep our attitudes in gratitude, our moods positive and optimistic, and our energy high.

4) The outlined values, standards, and vision that we have for our brand and business.

The culture meeting is more than just a new employee orientation. This is a one-day deep dive into who we are, where we're going, and what's expected of everyone on the team—myself included.

5) The Name-That-Tune Game

I'm honestly not sure how this one started, but every week or so I'll whistle or hum a random song to the team, and the first person to come up with the song title and artist gets a ten-dollar gift card to Starbucks. If I'm traveling I'll record my musical interlude on my smartphone and I'll send a group email to the team. The first person to respond to my email with the correct answer wins the gift card.

Are you catching on yet? Morale building infuses fun, lightheartedness, and play into the monotony of work. But make no mistake about it: As consistent as we are about keeping morale high and keeping things fun, we're also just as diligent about doing the work, doing it well, and exceeding expectations.

6) Monthly Birthday and Workaversary Parties

Once a month the team orders a group lunch on the company's dime and celebrates all of the birthdays and workaversaries for the month. The once-per-month party is done on a lunch break and is a welcome time to connect and enjoy a hot, catered lunch.

7) Team Yoga

The team members came up with this one, and Di started joining them, too. During their morning break, a big group of team members meet down in our learning center, dim the lights, turn on soothing music, and practice fifteen minutes of yoga together. They form a large circle on the carpet and go around the circle, taking turns leading the group in a pose, stretch, or exercise. No one is a true yogi—the moves are often variations of athletic stretches, boot camp exercises, popular yoga poses, and, when our nine-year-old, Chloe, is there, some very creative, funny poses! The group session ends with a quick cheer and everyone goes back to their work stations feeling great.

8) Annual FBBC Family BBQ

Every year at the beginning of summer, Di and I will host all the team members and their families on our one-acre property for an extravagant BBQ. We line our driveway with food trucks, pepper the yard with fancy white sofas, and fire up the slushy machine with frozen margaritas and champagne slushies! It's a wonderful time to connect with not only our team members, but also with their spouses, kids, and significant others. Their outside teams matter, too!

9) Annual Toys for Tots Event and Epic Holiday Party

One of my core values is to give back and to share my success with the less fortunate. During the holidays, this means supporting the Marine Toys for Tots drive, which gives presents to children who would otherwise wake up on Christmas morning with no gift to open. Every year I set aside $250,000, and we get our local Target store to close down on a particular morning in December to allow our team and their families to swarm the toy section, filling hundreds of shopping carts with toys for the local community that Toys for Tots serves. It's a magical, fun experience that we share as a team every year. Then that evening we party like it's 1999 at our annual holiday party.

10) Semiannual Self-Mastery Event

After burning through a few seasons of toxic employees, I began to look at my team members as assets to be invested in rather than adversaries to be resented. These smart, capable people are choosing to spend their time and energy on growing my business, so I decided that it was my duty to give back to them by way of usable, excel-at-life education. I am in the business of coaching entrepreneurs. It's my talent and a value that my employees also benefit from.

Twice a year I offer a nonmandatory self-improvement and self-mastery mastermind for team members. I've held this at my home, with Di cooking up a hot breakfast for everyone to enjoy while I teach, and I've also had other thought leaders and personal development experts come in to teach and edify my team in our learning center.

You're welcome to borrow some or all of these morale-boosting ideas to implement with your team, but my guess is that you'll ultimately come up with your own. The key is that you are making an effort to do something. Remember that your attitude toward your team members sets the flavor and the tone of your team morale. If you are muttering under your breath about them, then you can be sure that they are muttering under their breath about you, too. But if you approach them with love, respect, appreciation, and fun, then you will soon build a loyal, strong team.

EXERCISE

Take one of the ideas above and incorporate it into your team's rituals! How did it go?

Surprise your team members with an unexpected lunch and show them gratitude.

CONCLUSION: NEVER PEAK

I WOKE UP TODAY in a house I'm proud of. I spent time with my family without worrying whether I was taking time away from my business. I started my morning early—while most people were sleeping—and by the time they awoke, I got more done than I used to get done in weeks. I studied my vision and realized that, every day, I am getting closer to making it a reality.

I slept well last night. I woke up and ate clean, in a fashion that keeps my body nourished. I didn't wonder if I was going to have an anxiety attack. I don't have that kind of intense anxiety in my life anymore because I've eliminated everything that's not in line with my vision, and I have a team around me I can count on to help with the heavy lifting. Sure, I have stresses from time to time (who doesn't?), but I have the tools and techniques to deal with them. I'm happy, and even though I'm still charging hard, I come at it from a place of real joy.

When I went into the Fit Body Boot Camp headquarters, I didn't have to avoid anyone. I could look each person in the eye and know they were fighter jets; that they were there because they were rock stars; and that they were, each in their own way, making our business grow. I'm invested in their success, and they are invested in the success of Fit Body Boot Camp.

Speaking of which, Fit Body Boot Camp is on fire! We are well on our way to 2,500 locations. We're headed toward our big goal of helping one hundred million people worldwide reach their health and fitness goals. I'm proud to say that the business is massively profitable. But more important than profits, we're leaving a whole generation of people healthier than they've ever been. The dream that started for me as a young, struggling personal trainer twenty years ago evolved into an empire I'm proud to lead.

I had a couple calls with people today who inspire and challenge me. One of them runs a multimillion-dollar business; one of them advises the top CEOs in the world. Both are people who I consider part of my outside team, and I consider myself part of theirs. These are people who, just a few years ago, I would have never foreseen spending time with, because I didn't think of myself as in their league. I used to see myself as the immigrant kid from a Communist country. Now I see myself as an industry leader and mentor to up-and-coming entrepreneurs.

All of this happened because I manned up and did the work to improve my self-esteem and my self-image. It happened because I took responsibility for leading myself and my team. It happened because I got clear on my vision and the path to get there. And it happened because I worked at becoming a better communicator and faster decision-maker. It happened because I committed to building a team of high performers and holding myself and them to high standards and expectations.

I hope this book gave you a path to doing the same. Part of my goal in writing the book was to be as honest as possible: to give you a window into how low things can get for an entrepreneur when you choose to be undisciplined and fail to take your role as leader. You don't have to continue to suffer. Your business is not doomed. You can build yourself an empire. But first you must give up the excuses, take control of the situation, and rise to your potential. I didn't sugarcoat how hard this journey has been for me and how hard it will be for you, but I don't want to make it seem impossible. It wasn't and it isn't. And the journey is damn worth it.

I also don't just want you to read this book and then put it on a shelf and go back to how everything was before. Even today, I do the exercises in this book. Hell, I even did them while writing it. Writing was an anxiety-inducing process for me. I'd much rather create ten more multimillion-dollar businesses than write another book. But that's also why I'm going to write another book in the future. Like every other adversity in my life, I choose to get better at authoring a book and make it my super power.

The same can happen to you. If I can leave you with a final thought, it's this: Growth is perpetual. There is always room for more. Even today, I know I'm nowhere near the entrepreneur, father, husband, writer, leader, or friend I want to be. I've done a lot in my life, but I've got a lot of gas left in the tank—and I don't want to spend that energy reminiscing about the good times back when. I want to spend it creating new and powerful memories! In a little-remembered line from *The Sopranos*, Tony Soprano said, "'Remember when . . .' is the lowest form of conversation that any two people can have." Truer words have never spoken.

It doesn't matter what you did in high school, how great you were on the football team, or how impressive you were in your twenties. It doesn't matter what you did yesterday or before lunch. Talking about your glory days in the past tense is the best way to neuter your personal growth and future potential.

Who cares about what happened in the past? You're better off putting all of your focus and energy on creating your future and not settling for where you are now, or worse, where you used to be. Think of all the huge advancements and leaps we've taken as a society simply because of people who chose not to settle.

The United States would not have become the country it became had some folks decided that the king's way was the only way. Cars would not have evolved had everyone thought that Henry Ford had built the perfect form of transportation (and as Ford supposedly said, there never would have been a car if he had been happy with horses). Air travel would not exist had George Holt been satisfied with cars and trains as the only mode of travel.

You can see the mark that people who chose never to settle made on this world: from fashion to film, service to schools, weddings to warfare, food to fitness. Progress, change, achievement, and results come from those who choose never to settle and hold themselves to higher standards.

At the heart of manning up are two imperatives: Hold yourself to a high standard and achieve all that you're capable of as an entrepreneur and industry leader. From your health to your family to your relationships to your business, you're the one who determines what success looks like. You have the responsibility for how those things develop and turn out. And you can do the work—with the help of this book—to make your biggest and best dreams come true.

The big lesson I hope you take away is to never settle with "good enough." You always get what you tolerate. If you tolerate mediocrity, then that's what you'll get. Although this book is about entrepreneurial leadership, the lessons here will reach into every part of your life. If you choose to apply the lessons of decisiveness, clear communication, emotional resilience, clarity of vision, and building a team of fighter jets that you've learned from this book, then you will build a business that will become an industry titan—one that is massively profitable and fun to run. But as I said, make no mistake about it, this level of leadership will bleed into every aspect of your life and in the most positive of ways. You are a leader and it's time to step into your role. Leadership is about developing yourself first and everyone around you next into their fullest potential.

Never settle for good enough. Good enough is simply not good enough.

The moment you settle is the moment you lower your standards. The moment you settle is the moment when someone else will step up and make you obsolete and pick up where you left off. And if that's been you, or might be you, then it's time to man up.

That's the philosophy behind my motto: "Never peak—the best is yet to come." Even for me, the best is yet to come. You ain't seen nothing yet! I won't peak until I'm old and gray and just moments away from taking my last breath. The highest standard is all I'll take. And that's how I want you to live your life, run your business, and what I want you to expect of others (both personally and professionally).

I give you permission to man up, cut your excuses, take control, and reach your highest potential. There's still so much more out there for us all. I challenge you to raise your expectations. And I commit to you that I will raise mine, too!

GIVE YOURSELF PERMISSION

In closing, I would like to thank you for taking the time to read *Man Up*. I hope that you're chomping at the bit to man up in all areas of your life, and that you're able to derive value from the lessons and experiences that I've shared in these pages. Throughout the book you may have noticed that I "gave you permission" in several areas about several different topics.

Who am I to think that you need my permission to do anything?

I made those statements very intentionally, not because you need my permission, but because you need to grant *yourself* permission. So often we wait on the sidelines, waiting for someone, anyone, to give us permission to succeed or to let us know that it's okay to have high expectations and standards for ourselves and others. I decided to be that someone for you. But really, my friend, it is you alone who has the power to give yourself the permission to man up and, ultimately, to live the life you've always wanted.

Give yourself permission to grab hold of everything you've ever wanted in life.

Give yourself permission to live life on your own terms.

Give yourself permission to make as much money as you want.

Give yourself permission to not have to explain yourself.

Give yourself permission to think and dream bigger.

Give yourself permission to give up mediocrity in every area of your life.

Give yourself permission to increase your self-worth.

Give yourself permission to love yourself.

Give yourself permission to get what you want.

Give yourself permission to ignore what others say about you.

Give yourself permission to enjoy incredible experiences with your family.

Give yourself permission to be a capitalist.

Give yourself permission to build a reliable, loyal, hardworking team who fiercely guards your time, grows your money, and propels your momentum.

Give yourself permission to cut your deadlines in half.

Give yourself permission to not just be successful but to build an empire.

Give yourself permission to MAN UP!

ACKNOWLEDGMENTS

'D LIKE TO THANK my family, mentors, clients, team members, and of course my publisher, Glenn, as well as my editors, for your support, help, and patience. Thank you, Craig Ballantyne, Lewis Howes, Joan Arca, Ryan Holiday, and Jimmy Soni for your ongoing support and help in bringing this book to life.

Finally, I'd like to thank Howard Wasdin, retired Navy Seal, for writing his book, *Memoirs of an Elite Navy SEAL Sniper*. It was this book that led me to read eleven other books written by Navy Seals, and through these books I got to see the commonalities in what makes a great warrior, leader, and team member. Mr. Wasdin's book was published in 2011—this was the beginning times of the entrepreneurial struggles I was going through as I was building Fit Body Boot Camp and attempting to manage a fast-growing team. I was depressed, lost, and in massive debt at that time. I picked up Mr. Wasdin's book on a whim, to have something to read at night before bed as a form of distraction, to occupy my mind from my business troubles as I fell asleep.

Never did I imagine that one book about Navy Seals would lead to another book and then nine more. In these books about our great warriors, I discovered over and over the six pillars of leadership that I forced myself to learn and used to grow Fit Body Boot Camp and that I shared with you in this book. I've read several of these books repeatedly and without them I could not have evolved into the entrepreneur and leader I am today. Without evolving into the leader that I am today, I could not have built the businesses and made the impact in the industry that I serve.

Thank you, Howard Wasdin, Marcus Luttrell, Robert O'Neil, Jocko Willink, Leif Babin, Mark Owen, Adam Brown (RIP), Chris Kyle (RIP), Brandon Webb, Eric Greitens, William McRaven, and Rorke Denver. I thank you all for your service and sacrifice for our great country and for writing the books that not only helped make a leader out of me but allowed me to write this book for entrepreneurs worldwide.

ABOUT THE AUTHOR

 **Bedros Keuilian** is the founder and CEO of the Fit Body Boot Camp franchise as well as a sought-after speaker and business consultant. Keuilian is also an investor in more than a dozen companies ranging from subscription software platforms, digital ad agencies, franchising, and business coaching services.

Keuilian is the Immigrant Edge and American Dream, known as the hidden genius who entrepreneurs, bestselling authors, and thought leaders turn to when they want to turn their businesses into industry-leading empires.

Learn more about Bedros Keuilian at ManUp.com. While you're there, be sure to request your free leadership training course.